SQL MASTERY

A Complete Guide From Fundamentals to Advanced Techniques

Bukka Naga Swapna

CONTENTS

FOREWORD

SQL (Structured Query Language) has been the backbone of data management and manipulation for many years. It has been used extensively in a variety of industries, from finance to healthcare to e-commerce, and has become an essential skill for anyone looking to work with data. The demand for skilled SQL professionals continues to grow as businesses become increasingly reliant on data-driven insights to inform decision-making.

"SQL Mastery: A Complete Guide From Fundamentals to Advanced Techniques" provides a comprehensive look at the language, from its core SELECT statements to advanced topics like transactions and normalization. This book is designed to be a comprehensive resource for anyone looking to gain mastery over SQL, regardless of their prior experience with the language. Whether you're a beginner who has never written a SQL statement before or an experienced developer looking to deepen your understanding, this book has something for everyone.

With clear and concise explanations, numerous examples, and real-world scenarios, "SQL Mastery" will help you build a solid foundation in SQL, expand your skillset, and increase your ability to work with and manipulate data. The book covers all the essential topics, including SELECT statements, joins, database and table management, and data manipulation, as well as more advanced topics like optimization techniques, window functions, and common table expressions.

This book is not only a comprehensive resource, but also an engaging and accessible guide to SQL. The authors' passion for the subject shines through on every page, making the material both informative and enjoyable to read. By the end of the book, you will have a deep understanding of the language and the confidence to work with data in a variety of contexts.

So, whether you're a student, a professional, or simply someone looking to expand your knowledge of SQL, "SQL Mastery: A Complete Guide From Fundamentals to Advanced Techniques" is the perfect resource for you. I highly recommend it!

PREFACE

SQL (Structured Query Language) is the standard language for managing relational databases and it has been widely used in a variety of industries, including finance, healthcare, e-commerce, and many others. Whether you are a beginner or an experienced programmer, having a deep understanding of SQL is essential for your career growth.

SQL Mastery: A Complete Guide From Fundamentals to Advanced Techniques is a comprehensive guide to mastering SQL, from the basics to advanced topics. The book covers all the essential elements of SQL, starting with the SELECT statement, and moving on to more complex topics like JOINs, subqueries, and functions. The book also covers the administration of SQL databases, including the creation, deletion, and alteration of tables, and the backup of databases. The book concludes with a section on advanced topics such as transactions, normalization, optimization techniques, and many others.

This book is designed to provide a complete and in-depth understanding of SQL, taking you from a beginner to an expert level. The book is written in a clear and concise manner, making it easy to follow, even for those who have never worked with SQL before. Each chapter builds upon the knowledge gained in the previous chapter, gradually increasing the complexity of the topics covered.

Whether you are looking to learn SQL for the first time, or

you are an experienced programmer looking to upgrade your skills, SQL Mastery: A Complete Guide From Fundamentals to Advanced Techniques is the ideal resource for you. The book provides all the tools you need to achieve mastery of SQL, and to take your skills to the next level.

So, whether you are an aspiring data analyst, a database administrator, or a software developer, this book is your one-stop guide to SQL mastery. Get your copy today and start your journey to SQL mastery!

PROLOGUE

SQL, or Structured Query Language, is a powerful programming language used in the management and manipulation of relational databases. It is the most widely used language for data management and analysis, and a fundamental skill for any data professional.

In this book, "SQL Mastery: A Complete Guide from Fundamentals to Advanced Techniques," we explore the complexities and capabilities of this essential language. We begin with the basics of SQL SELECT statements, moving on to more advanced concepts such as SQL JOINS, database and table creation, and data manipulation techniques. Additionally, we delve into more advanced topics such as SQL constraints, normalization, optimization techniques, and much more.

Whether you are a beginner looking to learn SQL for the first time, or an experienced data professional seeking to expand your skills, this book offers a comprehensive guide to mastering SQL. Our step-by-step approach and clear explanations make it easy to understand even the most complex concepts. With real-world examples and practical exercises, you'll be able to apply what you learn immediately to your work.

So, come along on this journey to SQL mastery. Whether you're looking to improve your data analysis skills, manage a database, or prepare for a career in data, this book is an essential resource.

INTRODUCTION TO DATABASES AND SQL

Databases and SQL can be traced back to the 1960s, when computer scientists began developing methods for organizing and retrieving data in a more efficient and scalable way.

One of the earliest forms of databases was the hierarchical database, which was developed in the late 1960s by IBM. In this type of database, data was organized in a tree-like structure, with each node in the tree representing a record in the database. This type of database was well-suited to applications where data was highly structured and relationships between records were clear.

In the 1970s, a new type of database called the relational database was developed. The relational database was invented by Dr. E. F. Codd, who worked at IBM at the time. In a relational database, data is stored in tables, with each table representing a different type of data. The relational database also introduced the concept of relationships between tables, which allowed data from multiple tables to be combined in a single query.

The relational database was a significant step forward in the development of databases, and it led to the development of the Structured Query Language (SQL), which was designed specifically for working with relational databases. SQL is a declarative language, which means that users specify what they want the database to do, rather than how to do it. This makes SQL a powerful and flexible tool for working with databases, and it quickly became the standard language for working with relational databases.

Since the development of relational databases and SQL, there have been many advances in database technology, including the development of new types of databases such as NoSQL databases and the use of big data technologies to handle large amounts of data. Nevertheless, the relational database and SQL remain an important and widely-used technology, and they continue to play a critical role in the management and analysis of data in a wide range of applications and industries.

Types Of Dbms

1. Relational Database Management System (RDBMS):

A relational database management system (RDBMS) is a type of database management system that organizes data into one or more tables of rows and columns, where each table represents a specific type of data, such as customers, orders, or products. The relationships between the data are defined by using keys, which are unique values that identify each row in a table.

In a relational database, data is stored in tables, and each table has a unique name and a set of columns that define the types of data that can be stored in the table. The rows in a table represent individual instances of the data, such as a specific customer or a specific order.

One of the key advantages of a relational database is that it allows data to be related to one another in a meaningful way. For example, you can use keys to define relationships between customers and orders, so that you can retrieve all of the orders for a specific customer. You can also define relationships between tables, so that you can retrieve data from multiple tables with a single query.

Another advantage of a relational database is that it provides a flexible and scalable way to store data. You can add new tables, columns, and rows to a relational database as needed, and you can also modify the structure of the database to accommodate changes in the data. This makes relational databases well-suited for applications that need to store large amounts of data and support a wide range of data types.

SQL is the standard language used for interacting with relational databases, and most relational database management systems support SQL as the primary means of accessing and manipulating data stored in the database. By using SQL, you can create tables, insert data, retrieve data, update data, and delete data, as well as perform more complex operations such as aggregating data, joining data from multiple tables, and filtering data based on specific conditions.

2. Object-Relational Database Management System (ORDBMS):

An Object-Relational Database Management System (ORDBMS) is a type of database management system that combines the features of both a relational database management system (RDBMS) and an object-oriented programming (OOP) language. It is designed to store and manage complex data structures, such as object-oriented data types, and to support the development of complex applications.

In an ORDBMS, data is stored in tables just like in a relational database, but each table can also contain objects, which are collections of data and methods that define how the data can be manipulated. Objects in an ORDBMS are similar to objects in OOP languages like Java or C++, and they can be used to represent complex data structures, such as hierarchical relationships, geometric shapes, or multimedia data.

One of the key advantages of an ORDBMS is that it provides a more flexible and efficient way to store complex data structures than a traditional relational database. With an ORDBMS, you can store and manage data in a way that is more in line with how the data is used in your application, which can result in improved performance and reduced complexity.

Another advantage of an ORDBMS is that it provides a more powerful and flexible way to query and manipulate data than a traditional relational database. With an ORDBMS, you can use SQL to query and manipulate data, as well as OOP methods to define custom operations that can be performed on the data. This can make it easier to develop complex applications that require sophisticated data processing.

3. Hierarchical Database Management System (HDBMS):

A Hierarchical Database Management System (HDBMS) is a type of database management system that organizes data in a hierarchical tree-like structure, where each node in the hierarchy represents a record or a group of records. In an HDBMS, each node in the hierarchy can have one or more child nodes, and each child node can have only one parent node.

In an HDBMS, the relationships between nodes are established using parent-child links, which define the hierarchical structure of the data. Each node in the hierarchy can contain multiple fields, or attributes, which store the data values associated with that node.

One of the key advantages of an HDBMS is that it provides a natural and intuitive way to represent and manage hierarchical data, such as organizational charts, product catalogs, or geographic data. With an HDBMS, you can easily navigate and query the hierarchical structure of the data to retrieve specific records or groups of records.

Another advantage of an HDBMS is that it provides a simple and efficient way to maintain referential integrity, which is the property of ensuring that relationships between records are consistent and accurate. With an HDBMS, you can enforce referential integrity by defining parent-child links between nodes in the hierarchy, which prevent you from creating relationships that are inconsistent or that violate the constraints of the system.

4. Network Database Management System (NDBMS):

A Network Database Management System (NDBMS) is a type of database management system that organizes data in a network structure, where each record can have multiple relationships with other records. In a Network Database Management System (NDBMS), data is stored as a collection of interconnected records, where each record can have multiple relationships with other records.

In an NDBMS, relationships between records are established using pointers, which define the connectivity between records. Each record in the network can contain multiple fields, or attributes, which store the data values associated with that record.

One of the key advantages of an NDBMS is that it provides a flexible and scalable way to represent and manage complex data relationships, such as those found in customer-order-invoice systems, or in systems that manage interrelated data such as customers, suppliers, and products. With an NDBMS, you can easily navigate and query the network structure of the data to retrieve specific records or groups of records, based on the relationships between the records.

Another advantage of an NDBMS is that it provides a simple and efficient way to maintain referential integrity, which is the property of ensuring that relationships between records are consistent and accurate. With an NDBMS, you can enforce referential integrity by defining pointers between records, which prevent you from creating relationships that are inconsistent or that violate the constraints of the system.

5. NoSQL Database Management System (NDBMS):

NoSQL Database Management System (NDBMS) is a type of database management system that does not use the traditional structured query language (SQL) and instead uses non-relational data models, such as key-value, document, graph, or column-based, to store and manage data. NoSQL databases are designed to handle large amounts of unstructured or semi-structured data and to provide scalability, performance, and flexibility for modern web and mobile applications.

One of the key differences between NoSQL databases and traditional relational databases is that NoSQL databases do not enforce a fixed schema, which means that the structure of the data can change over time. This makes NoSQL databases ideal for handling large amounts of dynamic or evolving data, such as user-generated content, sensor data, or log data.

Another advantage of NoSQL databases is that they provide horizontal scalability, which means that they can handle large amounts of data and traffic by adding more nodes to the cluster. This makes NoSQL databases ideal for building large-scale, distributed, and fault-tolerant systems that can handle millions of requests per second.

NoSQL databases are also designed to handle complex and flexible data relationships, such as hierarchical, graph, or multi-valued relationships, that cannot be easily represented in a traditional relational database. This makes NoSQL databases ideal for use cases that require the ability to store and analyze large amounts of interconnected data, such as social networks, recommendation systems, or fraud detection systems.

6. Graph Database Management System (GDBMS):

A Graph Database Management System (GDBMS) is a type of NoSQL database management system that uses graph theory to store and manage data. Graph databases are designed to represent and store data as nodes and edges, which are relationships between the nodes.

Graph databases are particularly useful for handling data that has complex and interrelated relationships, such as social networks, recommendation systems, fraud detection systems, and customer relationship management systems. In these systems, data can be represented as entities and their relationships, making it easier to query, analyze, and visualize the data.

Graph databases differ from traditional relational databases and other NoSQL databases in that they are optimized for handling large numbers of relationships and for querying graph data. They use index-free adjacency, which allows them to retrieve related nodes in constant time, making them fast and efficient for graph traversal and analysis.

Graph databases also provide flexibility in handling data relationships. Unlike relational databases, which enforce a fixed schema, graph databases allow nodes and edges to be added, modified, or deleted dynamically, making it easier to handle changing data requirements.

Introduction To Sql

SQL (Structured Query Language) is a standardized programming language used for managing relational databases. A relational database is a collection of data that is organized into tables, with each table consisting of a set of rows and columns. SQL provides a way to interact with these relational databases, allowing users to perform tasks such as retrieving data, inserting new data, updating existing data, and deleting data.

SQL is an essential tool for anyone who works with data, as it provides a powerful and flexible way to access and manipulate large amounts of data. This makes SQL a valuable skill for data analysts, data scientists, database administrators, software developers, and many other professionals.

One of the key benefits of SQL is its declarative nature. This means that when you write an SQL statement, you specify what you want the database to do, and the database management system (DBMS) takes care of the details of how to perform the task. For example, if you want to retrieve a list of all employees who work in a particular department, you would write an SQL statement like this:

```
SELECT * FROM employees WHERE department = 'Marketing';
```

This statement tells the database to retrieve all columns (*) from the "employees" table where the "department" column is equal to "Marketing". The database management system takes care of the details of how to perform the task, such as how to retrieve the data from disk and how to filter the results based on the specified criteria.

Another benefit of SQL is that it is a standard language, which means that it is widely supported and used by many different database management systems. This makes SQL a portable language, which can be used to interact with a wide variety of databases, regardless of the underlying technology. This makes it easier for data professionals to work with different types of databases and to transfer their skills between different projects.

SQL is also a highly expressive language, which allows you to perform complex tasks with a single statement. For example, you can use SQL to aggregate data, perform mathematical calculations, and join data from multiple tables. This makes SQL a versatile tool that can be used to perform a wide range of data analysis and manipulation tasks.

CHAPTER 1: SQL SELECT (1)

SQL SELECT AND SELECT WHERE

SQL SELECT is used to retrieve data from one or more columns of a database table. The basic syntax for a SELECT statement is as follows:

```
SELECT column1, column2, column3, ...
FROM table_name;
```

In this syntax, **column1**, **column2**, **column3**, etc. are the names of the columns you want to retrieve data from, and **table_name** is the name of the table from which you want to retrieve the data.

For example, if you have a table named "employees" with columns **id**, **first_name**, **last_name**, and **salary**, you can retrieve all the data from the "**employees**" table

Table: employees

id	first_nam	last_name	salary

	e		
1	John	Luna	60000
2	David	Doe	40000
3	Smith	Robinson	70000
4	Millar	Rein	50000
5	Maria	Gracia	30000

by using the following SELECT statement:

```
SELECT id, first_name, last_name, salary
FROM employees;
```

This query will return the following result:

id	first_name	last_name	salary
1	John	Luna	60000
2	David	Doe	40000
3	Smith	Robinson	70000
4	Millar	Rein	50000
5	Maria	Gracia	30000

SQL SELECT WHERE is used to retrieve data from one or more columns of a database table based on a specific condition. The basic syntax for a SELECT WHERE statement is as follows:

```
SELECT column1, column2, column3, ...
FROM table_name
WHERE condition;
```

In this syntax, **column1**, **column2**, **column3**, etc. are the names of the columns you want to retrieve data from, **table_name** is the name of the table from which you want to retrieve the data, and **condition** is the condition that must be met for the data to be retrieved.

For example, if you have a table named "employees" with columns **id**, **first_name**, **last_name**, and **salary**, and you want to retrieve data for all employees with a salary greater than 50000, you can use the following SELECT WHERE statement:

```
SELECT id, first_name, last_name, salary
FROM employees
WHERE salary > 50000;
```

This query will return the following result:

id	first_name	last_name	salary
1	John	Luna	60000
3	Smith	Robinson	70000

Sql Operators

SQL Operators are symbols that perform specific operations on values and expressions in SQL. There are several types of SQL operators, including:

1. Arithmetic Operators: These operators perform arithmetic operations such as addition, subtraction, multiplication, and division. The arithmetic operators in SQL include '+', '-', '*', and '/'.

2. Comparison Operators: These operators are used to compare values in SQL. The comparison operators in SQL include '=', '<>', '<', '>', '<=', '>=', **'LIKE'**, **'IN'**, and **'BETWEEN'**.

3. Logical Operators: These operators are used to combine conditions in a query. The logical operators in SQL include **'AND'**, **'OR'**, and **'NOT'**.

4. Bitwise Operators: These operators perform bitwise operations on binary values. The bitwise operators in SQL include **'&'**, **'|'**, **'^'**, **'~'**, **'<<'**, and **'>>'**.

5. Concatenation Operators: These operators are used to concatenate strings in SQL. The concatenation operator in SQL is **'||'**.

6. Set Operators: These operators are used to combine the results of multiple SELECT statements. The set operators in SQL include **'UNION'**, **'INTERSECT'**, and **'EXCEPT'**.

7. Conditional Operators: These operators are used to conditionally return a value based on a specific condition. The conditional operator in SQL is **'CASE'**.

In SQL, operators are used in various clauses and statements, such as the WHERE clause, to filter data based on specific conditions, or in expressions to perform calculations. By using the appropriate operator, you can manipulate and retrieve data in a precise and efficient manner.

SQL AND, OR, AND NOT OPERATORS

SQL AND Operator

The SQL AND operator is a logical operator that is used to combine multiple conditions in a SQL query. The AND operator returns true only if both conditions are true. In other words, if one of the conditions is false, the result of the AND operator is false.

The syntax of the AND operator in SQL is:

```
SELECT column_name(s)
FROM table_name
WHERE condition1 AND condition2;
```

For example, suppose you have a table named **customers** with the following data:

id	name	city
1	Alice	Paris
2	Bob	London
3	Eve	Berlin
4	Dave	Paris

If you want to retrieve the data for all customers who live in Paris and have an id greater than 2, you can use the following SQL query:

```sql
SELECT *
FROM customers
WHERE city = 'Paris' AND id > 2;
```

This query will return the following result:

id	name	city
4	Dave	Paris

In this example, both conditions, **city = 'Paris'** and **id > 2**, must be true for the data to be returned. The AND operator ensures that only the data that meets both conditions is retrieved.

Sql Or Operator

The SQL OR operator is a logical operator that is used to combine multiple conditions in a SQL query. The OR operator returns true if at least one of the conditions is true. In other words, if one of the conditions is true, the result of the OR operator is true.

The syntax of the OR operator in SQL is:

```sql
SELECT column_name(s)
FROM table_name
WHERE condition1 OR condition2;
```

For example, suppose you have a table named **customers** with the following data:

id	name	city
1	Alice	Paris
2	Bob	London
3	Eve	Berlin
4	Dave	Paris

If you want to retrieve the data for all customers who live either in Paris or London, you can use the following SQL query:

```sql
SELECT *
FROM customers
WHERE city = 'Paris' OR city = 'London';
```

This query will return the following result:

id	name	city
1	Alice	Paris
2	Bob	London
4	Dave	Paris

In this example, either condition, **city = 'Paris'** or **city = 'London'**, must be true for the data to be returned. The OR operator ensures that the data that meets either condition is retrieved.

Combining Multiple Operators

In SQL, you can combine multiple operators to create complex conditions. For example, you can combine the "AND" and "OR" operators to create conditions that return data based on multiple criteria.

The following is an example of combining the "AND" and "OR" operators in a SQL query:

```
SELECT column_name(s)
FROM table_name
WHERE (condition1 AND condition2) OR condition3;
```

For example, suppose you have a table named **customers** with the following data:

id	name	city	age
1	Alice	Paris	25
2	Bob	London	30
3	Eve	Berlin	35
4	Dave	Paris	40

If you want to retrieve the data for all customers who are either 25 years old and live in Paris, or who are 35 years old, you can use the following SQL query:

```
SELECT *
FROM customers
WHERE (age = 25 AND city = 'Paris') OR age = 35;
```

This query will return the following result:

id	name	city	age
1	Alice	Paris	25

| 3 | Eve | Berlin | 35 |

In this example, either condition **(age = 25 AND city = 'Paris')** or **age = 35** must be true for the data to be returned. The combination of the "AND" and "OR" operators ensures that the data that meets either condition is retrieved.

Here's another example. Suppose you have a table named **orders** with the following data:

order_id	customer_name	product_name	quantity
1	John Doe	Phone	2
2	Jane Doe	Laptop	1
3	John Doe	Speaker	3
4	Jane Doe	Phone	1
5	John Doe	Headphones	4

If you want to retrieve the data for all orders that were placed by either John Doe or Jane Doe for a product quantity of either 2 or 3, you can use the following SQL query:

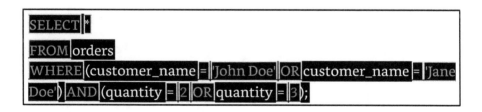

```
SELECT *
FROM orders
WHERE (customer_name = 'John Doe' OR customer_name = 'Jane Doe') AND (quantity = 2 OR quantity = 3);
```

This query will return the following result:

order_id	customer_name	product_name	quantity
1	John Doe	Phone	2

| 3 | John Doe | Speaker | 3 |

In this example, either condition **(customer_name = 'John Doe' OR customer_name = 'Jane Doe')** or **(quantity = 2 OR quantity = 3)** must be true for the data to be returned. The combination of the "AND" and "OR" operators ensures that the data that meets either condition is retrieved.

SQL SELECT DISTINCT

The **SELECT DISTINCT** statement in SQL is used to return only unique values from a table. When used in a query, it eliminates any duplicate rows from the result set.

For example, consider a table named **products** with the following data:

product_id	product_name	price
1	Phone	500
2	Laptop	1000
3	Speaker	150
4	Headphones	50
5	Phone	500

If you want to retrieve a list of all unique product names from the table, you can use the following SQL query:

```sql
SELECT DISTINCT product_name
FROM products;
```

This query will return the following result:

product_name

Phone
Laptop
Speaker
Headphones

In this example, the **SELECT DISTINCT** statement eliminates the duplicate values in the **product_name** column, and only returns the unique values.

Here's another example of using the **SELECT DISTINCT** statement in SQL.

Consider a table named **employees** with the following data:

employee_id	first_name	last_name	department
1	John	Doe	Sales
2	Jane	Doe	Marketing
3	John	Smith	Sales
4	Jane	Doe	Marketing

If you want to retrieve a list of all unique departments in the **employees** table, you can use the following SQL query:

```
SELECT DISTINCT department
FROM employees;
```

This query will return the following result:

department
Sales
Marketing

In this example, the **SELECT DISTINCT** statement eliminates the duplicate values in the **department** column, and only returns the unique values.

Distinct With Count

The **COUNT** function can be used with the **DISTINCT** keyword to count only the unique values in a particular column.

For example, consider a table named **employees** with the following data:

employee_id	first_name	last_name	department
1	John	Doe	Sales
2	Jane	Doe	Marketing
3	John	Smith	Sales
4	Jane	Doe	Marketing

To count the number of unique departments in the **employees** table, you can use the following SQL query:

```sql
SELECT COUNT(DISTINCT department)
FROM employees;
```

This query will return the following result:

COUNT(DISTINCT department)
2

In this example, the **COUNT** function is used to count the number of unique departments in the **department** column, which is 2.

SQL SELECT AS

The **AS** keyword in SQL allows you to assign an alias to a column name in a SELECT statement. The alias acts as a substitute for the actual column name and can be used to simplify or clarify the output of the query.

For example, consider a table named **employees** with the following data:

employee_id	first_name	last_name	department
1	John	Doe	Sales
2	Jane	Doe	Marketing
3	John	Smith	Sales
4	Jane	Doe	Marketing

To select the first name and last name columns and display them with labels "First Name" and "Last Name", respectively, you can use the following SQL query:

```
SELECT first_name AS "First Name", last_name AS "Last Name"
FROM employees;
```

This query will return the following result:

First Name	Last Name
John	Doe
Jane	Doe
John	Smith
Jane	Doe

In this example, the **AS** keyword is used to assign the alias "First Name" to the **first_name** column and "Last Name" to the **last_name** column. The result of the query will display the data with the alias names instead of the actual column names.

SQL AS With Expression

The **AS** keyword can also be used in conjunction with expressions to display calculated values in a SELECT statement. Expressions are a combination of operators, functions, and column names that produce a single value.

For example, consider a table named **employees** with the following data:

employee_id	first_name	last_name	salary
1	John	Doe	50000
2	Jane	Doe	55000
3	John	Smith	60000
4	Jane	Doe	65000

To select the first name, last name, and a calculated salary column with a 10% raise, you can use the following SQL query:

```
SELECT first_name, last_name, salary * 1.1 AS "Salary with 10% Raise"
FROM employees;
```

This query will return the following result:

first_name	last_name	Salary with 10% Raise
John	Doe	55000
Jane	Doe	60500
John	Smith	66000
Jane	Doe	71500

In this example, the **salary * 1.1** expression is used to calculate the salary with a 10% raise, and the **AS "Salary with 10% Raise"** clause assigns the alias "Salary with 10% Raise" to the calculated expression. The result of the query will display the data with the calculated values and the assigned alias names.

SQL LIMIT, TOP AND FETCH FIRST

Sql Limit

The **LIMIT** clause in SQL is used to limit the number of rows returned by a SELECT statement. It is often used in conjunction with the **ORDER BY** clause to return a specific number of rows starting from a specific row. The **LIMIT** clause is supported by most relational database management systems including MySQL, PostgreSQL, and SQL Server.

Here's an example of how to use the **LIMIT** clause. Consider a table named **employees** with the following data:

employee_id	first_name	last_name	salary
1	John	Doe	50000
2	Jane	Doe	55000
3	John	Smith	60000
4	Jane	Doe	65000

To select the first two rows from the **employees** table, you can use the following SQL query:

```
SELECT * FROM employees
LIMIT 2;
```

This query will return the following result:

```
| employee_id | first_name | last_name | salary |
|-------------|------------|-----------|--------|
| 1           | John       | Doe       | 50000  |
| 2           | Jane       | Doe       | 55000  |
```

Here is an example of how you can use the **TOP** keyword in SQL:

```
SELECT TOP 3 * FROM employees;
```

This query will return the first three rows from the **employees** table:

```
| employee_id | first_name | last_name | salary |
|-------------|------------|-----------|--------|
| 1           | John       | Doe       | 50000  |
| 2           | Jane       | Doe       | 55000  |
| 3           | Bob        | Smith     | 45000  |
```

Note that the order of the rows returned by the query is not guaranteed unless you specify an "**ORDER BY**" clause.

Fetch First Clause

The **FETCH FIRST** clause is a standard SQL syntax used to limit the number of rows returned by a query. It works similarly to the **LIMIT** and **TOP** keywords.

Here is an example of how you can use the **FETCH FIRST** clause in SQL:

```
SELECT * FROM employees FETCH FIRST 3 ROWS ONLY;
```

This query will return the first three rows from the **employees** table:

```
| employee_id | first_name | last_name | salary  |
|-------------|------------|-----------|---------|
| 1           | John       | Doe       | 50000   |
| 2           | Jane       | Doe       | 55000   |
| 3           | Bob        | Smith     | 45000   |
```

Note that the order of the rows returned by the query is not guaranteed unless you specify an **"ORDER BY"** clause.

SQL IN OPERATOR

The **IN** operator in SQL is used to determine whether a specified value matches any value in a list or subquery.

Here is an example of how you can use the **IN** operator in SQL:

Suppose we have a table **orders** with the following data:

```
+------------+------------+---------+
| order_id   | customer_id| product |
+------------+------------+---------+
| 1          | 1001       | Phone   |
| 2          | 1002       | Laptop  |
| 3          | 1003       | TV      |
| 4          | 1001       | Tablet  |
| 5          | 1002       | Phone   |
+------------+------------+---------+
```

We can use the **IN** operator to find all orders made by customers with customer IDs 1001 or 1002:

```
SELECT *
FROM orders
WHERE customer_id IN (1001, 1002);
```

The result of this query will be:

```
+--------------+--------------+---------+
| order_id     | customer_id| product |
+--------------+--------------+---------+
| 1            | 1001         | Phone   |
| 2            | 1002         | Laptop  |
| 5            | 1002         | Phone   |
+--------------+--------------+---------+
```

SQL BETWEEN OPERATOR

The **SQL BETWEEN** operator is used to filter data based on a specified range of values. The BETWEEN operator can be used with numeric, date, and text values.

Here is an example using the BETWEEN operator to filter data from a new table called "Orders". This table contains information about customer orders, including the order date and the total amount of the order:

```
SELECT *
FROM Orders
WHERE OrderAmount BETWEEN 100 AND 500;
```

This query will return all rows from the "Orders" table where the value in the "OrderAmount" column is between 100 and 500. In other words, it will return all orders with a total amount between $100 and $500. The result will look something like this:

```
OrderID | CustomerID | OrderDate | OrderAmount
---------------------------------------------------
1       | 123        | 2020-01-01| 300
2       | 124        | 2020-02-01| 200
3       | 125        | 2020-03-01| 400
4       | 126        | 2020-04-01| 500
```

As you can see, the query returns all rows where the

"OrderAmount" is between 100 and 500, inclusive.

Sql Is Null And Not Null

The SQL IS NULL and NOT NULL operators are used to test for NULL values in a database table. A NULL value represents an absence of a value in a database column, which is different from a value of zero or an empty string.

here's an example of practical uses for IS NULL and NOT NULL in SQL.

Consider a table called "employees" with the following data:

```
+----+--------+--------+---------+
| id | name   | salary | manager |
+----+--------+--------+---------+
| 1  | John   | 5000   | NULL    |
| 2  | Sarah  | 6000   | 1       |
| 3  | Michael| 7000   | 1       |
| 4  | David  | 6000   | 2       |
+----+--------+--------+---------+
```

The "manager" column specifies the id of the manager of each employee. If the value is NULL, it means that the employee does not have a manager.

Example 1: Using IS NULL

```
SELECT name
FROM employees
WHERE manager IS NULL;
```

This query will return the names of all employees who do not have a manager:

```
+------+
| name |
+------+
| John |
+------+
```

Example 2: Using NOT NULL

```
SELECT name
FROM employees
WHERE manager IS NOT NULL;
```

This query will return the names of all employees who have a manager:

```
+--------+
| name   |
+--------+
| Sarah  |
| Michael|
| David  |
+--------+
```

In this way, you can use IS NULL and NOT NULL operators to filter the results based on whether a column contains a NULL value or not.

SQL MIN() AND MAX()

SQL MIN() and **MAX()** are two aggregate functions in SQL that are used to determine the minimum and maximum value in a set of data, respectively.

MIN(): The MIN() function returns the minimum value from the specified column. For example, consider the following "employees" table:

```
+----+----------+----------+
| id | name     | salary   |
+----+----------+----------+
| 1  | John     | 5000     |
| 2  | Jane     | 6000     |
| 3  | Tom      | 4000     |
| 4  | Sarah    | 7000     |
+----+----------+----------+
```

To find the minimum salary from the "employees" table, you can use the following SQL query:

```
SELECT MIN(salary) as minimum_salary
FROM employees;
```

This query will return the following result:

```
+-------------------+
| minimum_salary    |
+-------------------+
| 4000              |
+-------------------+
```

MAX(): The MAX() function returns the maximum value from the specified column. For example, consider the following "employees" table:

```
+----+---------+----------+
| id | name    | salary   |
+----+---------+----------+
| 1  | John    | 5000     |
| 2  | Jane    | 6000     |
| 3  | Tom     | 4000     |
| 4  | Sarah   | 7000     |
+----+---------+----------+
```

To find the maximum salary from the "employees" table, you can use the following SQL query:

```
SELECT MAX(salary) as maximum_salary
FROM employees;
```

This query will return the following result:

```
+------------------+
| maximum_salary   |
+------------------+
| 7000             |
+------------------+
```

SQL COUNT()

The SQL COUNT() function is used to count the number of rows in a specific column or the entire table. It returns the number of rows in a table that match the specified condition. The syntax for the COUNT() function is as follows:

```
SELECT COUNT(column_name)
FROM table_name
WHERE condition;
```

Where "column_name" is the name of the column you want to count, "table_name" is the name of the table, and "condition" is an optional WHERE clause to specify the rows you want to count. If you don't specify a column name, the function will count all rows in the table.

For example, if you have a table named "employees" and you want to count the number of employees in the table, you can use the following SQL query:

```
SELECT COUNT(*)
FROM employees;
```

This query will return the total number of rows in the "employees" table. If you only want to count the number of employees in the "department" column, you can use the following query:

```
SELECT COUNT(department)
FROM employees;
```

This query will return the number of non-null values in the "department" column.

here is an example of using the COUNT() function in SQL:

Let's say you have a table named "employees" with columns "id", "name", "department", and "salary". If you want to count the number of employees in the department "Sales", you can use the following SQL query:

```
SELECT COUNT(*)
FROM employees
WHERE department = 'Sales';
```

This query will return the number of employees in the "Sales" department. For example, if there are 10 employees in the "Sales" department, the query will return **10**.

SQL SUM() AND AVG()

SQL SUM() and **AVG()** are aggregate functions in SQL that allow you to perform calculations on columns of data in a table.

let's consider a table named "orders" which contains the following data:

```
+----+---------+-------+
| ID | Item    | Price |
+----+---------+-------+
| 1  | Phone   | 500   |
| 2  | Laptop  | 1000  |
| 3  | Tablet  | 700   |
| 4  | Headset | 200   |
| 5  | Monitor | 800   |
+----+---------+-------+
```

Example 1: Using SUM() function to get the total of all the prices in the "orders" table:

```
SELECT SUM(Price) as Total_Price FROM orders;
```

This query will return the following result:

```
+--------------+
| Total_Price  |
+--------------+
| 3300         |
+--------------+
```

Example 2: Using AVG() function to get the average price of all the items in the "orders" table:

```
SELECT AVG(Price) as Average_Price FROM orders;
```

This query will return the following result:

```
+----------------+
| Average_Price  |
+----------------+
| 660            |
+----------------+
```

These aggregate functions can also be combined with other SQL clauses, such as GROUP BY, to perform more complex calculations and analysis of data in a table.

CHAPTER 2: SQL SELECT (II)

SQL ORDER BY

The **ORDER BY** clause is used in SQL to sort the result set of a query in ascending or descending order based on one or more columns. The syntax for the **ORDER BY** clause is as follows:

```
SELECT column1, column2, ...
FROM table_name
ORDER BY column1 [ASC | DESC], column2 [ASC | DESC], ...;
```

The **ORDER BY** clause sorts the result set based on the values in the specified columns. The optional **ASC** keyword specifies that the result set should be sorted in ascending order (which is the default), while the **DESC** keyword specifies that the result set should be sorted in descending order.

Here's an example to illustrate the use of the **ORDER BY** clause. Consider a table named **employees** with the following data:

```
+----+----------+--------+--------+
| id | name     | salary | city   |
+----+----------+--------+--------+
| 1  | John Doe | 50000  | London |
| 2  | Jane Doe | 55000  | Paris  |
| 3  | Bob Smith| 45000  | Berlin |
| 4  | Alice    | 60000  | Madrid |
+----+----------+--------+--------+
```

To sort the **employees** table in ascending order based on the salary column, you can use the following SQL query:

```sql
SELECT *
FROM employees
ORDER BY salary;
```

This query will return the following result:

```
+----+----------+--------+--------+
| id | name     | salary | city   |
+----+----------+--------+--------+
| 3  | Bob Smith| 45000  | Berlin |
| 1  | John Doe | 50000  | London |
| 2  | Jane Doe | 55000  | Paris  |
| 4  | Alice    | 60000  | Madrid |
+----+----------+--------+--------+
```

To sort the **employees** table in descending order based on the salary column, you can use the following SQL query:

```sql
SELECT *
FROM employees
ORDER BY salary DESC;
```

This query will return the following result:

```
+----+-----------+--------+--------+
| id | name      | salary | city   |
+----+-----------+--------+--------+
| 4  | Alice     | 60000  | Madrid |
| 2  | Jane Doe  | 55000  | Paris  |
| 1  | John Doe  | 50000  | London |
| 3  | Bob Smith | 45000  | Berlin |
+----+-----------+--------+--------+
```

SQL GROUP BY

SQL GROUP BY clause is used in conjunction with aggregate functions to group the data from one or more columns based on the values in those columns. The GROUP BY clause is placed after the WHERE clause in a SELECT statement and is used to group rows that have the same values in the specified columns into summary rows.

For example, consider the following table named "sales":

SaleID	ProductID	Quantity	Price
1	101	5	10
2	102	3	20
3	101	2	10
4	102	4	20

To get the total quantity of each product sold, we can use the following query:

```
SELECT ProductID, SUM(Quantity)
FROM sales
GROUP BY ProductID;
```

This query will return the following result:

ProductID	SUM(Quantity)

101	7
102	7

The query groups the sales data by the **ProductID** column and returns the total quantity of each product sold by using the SUM aggregate function. The result shows that product 101 was sold in a quantity of 7, and product 102 was sold in a quantity of 7 as well.

Here's another example using the **GROUP BY** clause:

Suppose you have a table named "orders" that stores information about the products that customers have ordered:

```
order_id | customer_id | product | quantity | price
-----------------------------------------------------------
1        | 1           | Phone     | 2        | 800
2        | 2           | Laptop    | 1        | 1200
3        | 3           | Tablet    | 3        | 500
4        | 1           | Headphone | 1        | 100
5        | 2           | Phone     | 1        | 800
```

You can use the following SQL query to find the total sales of each product:

```
SELECT product, SUM(price * quantity) AS total_sales
FROM orders
GROUP BY product;
```

This query will return the following result:

```
product    |  total_sales
- - - - - - - - - - - - - - - - - - - - - - - - - - - - - - - -
Headphone  |  100
Laptop     |  1200
Phone      |  1600
Tablet     |  1500
```

In this example, the **GROUP BY** clause is used to group the rows based on the **product** column. The **SUM** function is used to calculate the total sales of each product.

SQL LIKE

The SQL LIKE operator is used to match text string patterns. It is often used in conjunction with the SELECT, UPDATE, and DELETE statements. The LIKE operator uses two wildcard characters, the percent sign (%) and the underscore (_), to match patterns.

The percent sign matches any number of characters (including zero characters), while the underscore matches exactly one character.

For example, the following SQL query will retrieve all rows from a table called "employees" where the name column starts with the letter "J":

```
SELECT * FROM employees WHERE name LIKE 'J%';
```

In this example, the % sign matches any characters that come after the letter "J". So, the query will return all rows where the name column starts with the letter "J".

Another example:

```
SELECT * FROM employees WHERE name LIKE '_a%';
```

In this example, the _ sign matches exactly one character, and the % sign matches any characters that come after it. So, the query will return all rows where the name column starts with the second character being "a".

SQL WILDCARDS

SQL wildcards are characters used to search for patterns in data. These wildcards are used in conjunction with the LIKE operator to perform pattern matching. There are two wildcards in SQL:

Percentage Wildcard (%)

The percentage wildcard (%) is a special character used in SQL to match zero or more characters in a string. The % wildcard can be used in the SQL **LIKE** operator to search for a pattern in data.

For example, consider a table named **employees** with the following data:

```
+----+---------+--------+
| ID | Name    | Salary |
+----+---------+--------+
| 1  | John    | 5000   |
| 2  | Michael | 6000   |
| 3  | Brian   | 7000   |
| 4  | David   | 8000   |
| 5  | Tom     | 9000   |
+----+---------+--------+
```

To search for all employees whose name starts with "B", you can use the following SQL query:

```
SELECT * FROM employees
WHERE Name LIKE 'B%';
```

This query will return the following result:

```
+----+-------+--------+
| ID | Name  | Salary |
+----+-------+--------+
| 3  | Brian | 7000   |
+----+-------+--------+
```

As you can see, the query returns only one row for the employee named "Brian", whose name starts with "B".

Underscore Wildcard (_):

The underscore wildcard (_) in SQL is used to match any single character in a string. This operator can be used in the LIKE operator, which is used to search for a specific pattern in a string.

For example, if you have a table of employees and you want to search for all employees whose first name starts with the letter "J", you could use the following query:

```
SELECT *
FROM employees
WHERE first_name LIKE 'J_%';
```

In this example, the underscore represents any single character, so the query would return all employees whose first name starts with the letter "J" followed by any other single character.

Similarly, you could use the underscore wildcard to match any single digit in a string, like this:

```
SELECT *
FROM employees
WHERE salary LIKE '_0,000';
```

This query would return all employees whose salary ends with the pattern "0,000".

SQL UNION

The SQL UNION operator is used to combine the results of two or more SELECT statements into a single result set. This operator allows you to retrieve data from multiple tables as if they were a single table. The SELECT statements used in the UNION must have the same number of columns and the same data type for each corresponding column. The columns must also be in the same order in each SELECT statement.

Here's an example:

```
SELECT column1, column2, column3
FROM table1
UNION
SELECT column1, column2, column3
FROM table2;
```

In this example, the UNION operator combines the results of the two SELECT statements and returns a single result set containing all the rows from both tables.

It's important to note that the UNION operator removes any duplicate rows from the result set. If you want to include duplicates, you can use the UNION ALL operator instead.

Here's a practical example of using the SQL UNION operator:

Suppose we have two tables named "students" and "teachers",

and each table has columns "id", "name", and "age".

```
students table:
+----+-------+-----+
| id | name  | age |
+----+-------+-----+
|  1 | Alice |  22 |
|  2 | Bob   |  25 |
|  3 | Eve   |  28 |
+----+-------+-----+

teachers table:
+----+-------+-----+
| id | name  | age |
+----+-------+-----+
|  4 | John  |  35 |
|  5 | Sarah |  32 |
+----+-------+-----+
```

If we want to combine the data from both tables and retrieve the "id", "name", and "age" of all individuals (students and teachers), we can use the SQL UNION operator as follows:

```
SELECT id, name, age
FROM students
UNION
SELECT id, name, age
FROM teachers;
```

This will return the following result:

```
+----+--------+-----+
| id | name   | age |
+----+--------+-----+
|  1 | Alice  |  22 |
|  2 | Bob    |  25 |
|  3 | Eve    |  28 |
|  4 | John   |  35 |
|  5 | Sarah  |  32 |
+----+--------+-----+
```

Note that the UNION operator combines the data from the two tables and eliminates any duplicates.

SQL SUBQUERY

SQL subqueries are queries that are nested within other queries. The inner query, or subquery, executes first and its results are used in the execution of the outer query. Subqueries can be used in a variety of contexts, such as in the SELECT, FROM, WHERE, and HAVING clauses.

A subquery is always enclosed within parentheses, and it can be used to return a single value or multiple values.

Here's an example of using a subquery in the SELECT clause to retrieve the names of employees who earn more than the average salary of all employees:

```
SELECT first_name, last_name
FROM employees
WHERE salary > (SELECT AVG(salary) FROM employees);
```

In this example, the subquery **(SELECT AVG(salary) FROM employees)** calculates the average salary of all employees and returns it as a single value. The outer query then uses this value in its **WHERE** clause to filter the employees who earn more than the average salary.

Subqueries can also be used in the **FROM** clause to create derived tables, which can then be used in the outer query.

Subqueries can greatly simplify complex SQL statements, and they are an essential tool for querying databases.

Consider a scenario where we have two tables in our database: "employees" and "departments". The "employees" table has information about each employee in the company, including their name, employee ID, department ID, and salary. The "departments" table has information about each department, including the department name and the department ID.

We want to retrieve a list of employees who work in the "Sales" department. To do this, we can use a subquery. The subquery will return the department ID for the "Sales" department, and the main query will use this department ID to retrieve information about the employees who work in that department.

Here's an example of how we can write this subquery in SQL:

```
SELECT name, employee_id, salary

FROM employees

WHERE department_id = (SELECT department_id FROM departments WHERE department_name = 'Sales');
```

This query will return a list of employees who work in the "Sales" department, including their name, employee ID, and salary. The subquery **(SELECT department_id FROM departments WHERE department_name = 'Sales')** returns the department ID for the "Sales" department, and the main query uses this department ID to retrieve information about the employees who work in that department.

SQL ANY AND ALL

SQL ANY and ALL are operators that are used with a subquery in the WHERE clause of a SELECT, INSERT, UPDATE, or DELETE statement.

SQL ANY is used to compare a value with a single-row result of a subquery. It returns true if the comparison is true for any of the rows returned by the subquery.

For example, suppose you have a table named "orders" that contains information about customer orders, and a table named "customers" that contains information about customers. To find customers who have placed any order with a total amount greater than 1000, you can use the following SQL query:

```
SELECT customers.first_name, customers.last_name
FROM customers
WHERE 1000 < ANY (SELECT total_amount
                  FROM orders
                  WHERE orders.customer_id = customers.customer_id);
```

SQL ALL is used to compare a value with all values in a subquery. It returns true if the comparison is true for all of the rows returned by the subquery.

For example, to find customers who have placed all orders with a total amount greater than 1000, you can use the following SQL query:

```sql
SELECT customers.first_name, customers.last_name
FROM customers
WHERE 1000 < ALL (SELECT total_amount
                  FROM orders
                  WHERE orders.customer_id = customers.customer_id);
```

Note that the subquery in the above example must return at least one row in order for the query to return any results.

SQL CASE

The SQL CASE statement is a powerful tool used in SQL to return a value based on a series of conditions. The basic structure of the CASE statement is as follows:

```
CASE
WHEN condition1 THEN result1
WHEN condition2 THEN result2
...
ELSE resultN
END
```

The **CASE** statement starts with the keyword **CASE**, followed by one or more **WHEN** clauses. Each **WHEN** clause consists of a condition and a result that should be returned if the condition is met. The **ELSE** clause is optional and provides a default result if none of the conditions in the **WHEN** clauses are met.

Here is an example of a SQL query that uses a CASE statement to categorize employees based on their salaries:

```
SELECT employee_name, salary,
CASE
    WHEN salary < 5000 THEN 'Low'
    WHEN salary >= 5000 AND salary < 10000 THEN 'Mid'
    ELSE 'High'
END AS salary_category
FROM employees;
```

This query returns a table with the name, salary, and salary category of each employee, where the salary category is determined by the **CASE** statement. If an employee's salary is less than 5000, the **CASE** statement returns the value 'Low'; if the salary is between 5000 and 10000, it returns 'Mid'; and if the salary is greater than or equal to 10000, it returns 'High'.

Here is another example of using the SQL CASE statement in a SELECT query:

```sql
SELECT
  name,
  salary,
  CASE
    WHEN salary >= 100000 THEN 'Highly Paid'
    WHEN salary >= 50000 THEN 'Moderately Paid'
    ELSE 'Lowly Paid'
  END AS salary_group
FROM employees;
```

This query will return a result set like the following:

```
name          | salary  | salary_group
------------- |---------|-----------------
John Doe      | 90000   | Moderately Paid
Jane Doe      | 110000  | Highly Paid
Bob Smith     | 70000   | Moderately Paid
Alice Johnson | 80000   | Moderately Paid
```

SQL HAVING

The SQL HAVING clause is used to filter the results of a SELECT, UPDATE, INSERT, or DELETE statement based on aggregate values. The HAVING clause works in a similar way to the WHERE clause, but instead of filtering rows based on individual column values, it filters groups of rows defined by the GROUP BY clause.

For example, consider the following **employees** table:

```
+----+---------+--------+-------------+
| ID | name    | salary | city        |
+----+---------+--------+-------------+
| 1  | John    | 5000   | New York    |
| 2  | Michael | 6000   | Los Angeles |
| 3  | David   | 5500   | New York    |
| 4  | Sarah   | 7000   | Los Angeles |
| 5  | William | 8000   | New York    |
+----+---------+--------+-------------+
```

If you want to retrieve the average salary for each city and only display the cities where the average salary is greater than 6000, you can use the following SQL statement:

```
SELECT city, AVG(salary)
FROM employees
GROUP BY city
HAVING AVG(salary) > 6000;
```

This query will return the following result:

```
+-----------+------------+
| city      | AVG(salary) |
+-----------+------------+
| Los Angeles | 7000     |
| New York    | 7000     |
+-----------+------------+
```

SQL EXISTS

The SQL EXISTS operator is used to test the existence of any record in a subquery. It returns either "TRUE" or "FALSE". The subquery is executed only once to determine if at least one row is returned.

The general syntax for using the EXISTS operator is:

```
SELECT column(s)
FROM table1
WHERE EXISTS (SELECT column(s)
              FROM table2
              WHERE condition);
```

Here, "table1" is the outer query and "table2" is the inner query. The condition in the inner query is used to determine if any row exists in "table2". If a row exists, the EXISTS operator will return "TRUE" and the outer query will retrieve the columns specified.

Consider a scenario where you have two tables: "employees" and "orders". You want to retrieve all employees who have placed an order. You can use the following SQL query to achieve this:

```
SELECT first_name, last_name
FROM employees
WHERE EXISTS (SELECT *
              FROM orders
              WHERE employees.employee_id = orders.employee_id);
```

This query will return all employees who have placed an order by checking if the **employee_id** in the "employees" table exists in the "orders" table. The result of this query would be the first name and last name of the employees who have placed an order.

Here is another example of SQL EXISTS

Consider the following table, named "orders":

```
order_id | customer_name | order_date  | amount
---------------------------------------------------
1        | John Doe      | 2020-01-01  | 100
2        | Jane Doe      | 2020-01-02  | 150
3        | John Doe      | 2020-01-03  | 200
4        | Jane Doe      | 2020-01-04  | 175
5        | John Doe      | 2020-01-05  | 225
```

The following SQL query will use the **EXISTS** operator to check if there is any order placed by John Doe:

```
SELECT customer_name
FROM orders
WHERE EXISTS (
  SELECT *
  FROM orders
  WHERE customer_name = 'John Doe'
);
```

This query will return the following result:

```
customer_name
--------------
John Doe
John Doe
John Doe
```

As you can see, the query returns all the orders placed by John Doe, which means that the **EXISTS** operator has returned a **TRUE** value.

CHAPTER 3:
SQL JOINS

SQL JOIN is used to combine data from two or more tables based on a related column between them. The related column is called the "join condition" and is used to match rows from one table to rows from the other table. There are several types of SQL JOINS, including:

1. INNER JOIN: Returns only the rows that have matching values in both tables.

2. LEFT JOIN (or LEFT OUTER JOIN): Returns all the rows from the left table (table1), and the matching rows from the right table (table2). The result will contain unmatched rows from the right table, with NULL values.

3. RIGHT JOIN (or RIGHT OUTER JOIN): Returns all the rows from the right table (table2), and the matching rows from the left table (table1). The result will contain unmatched rows from the left table, with NULL values.

4. FULL OUTER JOIN: Returns all rows from both tables. The result will contain unmatched rows from both tables, with NULL values.

SQL INNER JOIN

The INNER JOIN is one of the most commonly used SQL JOINs. It returns only the rows that have matching values in both tables. For example, if we have two tables, "Customers" and "Orders", and we want to retrieve all orders made by customers, we can use the following SQL statement:

```
SELECT Customers.CustomerName, Orders.OrderID
FROM Customers
INNER JOIN Orders
ON Customers.CustomerID = Orders.CustomerID;
```

In this example, the INNER JOIN clause joins the two tables based on the values in the "CustomerID" column. The result set includes only those rows where there is a match between the values in the "CustomerID" column of both tables. The SELECT statement retrieves the "CustomerName" and "OrderID" columns from both tables, and the result will be a list of all orders made by each customer.

Practical example: Consider the following two tables

```
Table: Customers
+----+----------+-----+
| ID | Name     | Age |
+----+----------+-----+
| 1  | John Doe | 25  |
| 2  | Jane Doe | 30  |
| 3  | Jim Brown| 35  |
+----+----------+-----+

Table: Orders
+----+----------+----------+
| ID | OrderNo  | CustomerID |
+----+----------+----------+
| 1  | 1001     | 1        |
| 2  | 1002     | 2        |
| 3  | 1003     | 2        |
| 4  | 1004     | 3        |
+----+----------+----------+
```

A practical example of SQL INNER JOIN can be to retrieve the customer name and order number of all orders placed by customers. This can be achieved by using the following query:

```sql
SELECT Customers.Name, Orders.OrderNo
FROM Customers
INNER JOIN Orders
ON Customers.ID = Orders.CustomerID;
```

This query will return the following result:

```
+----------+--------+
| Name     | OrderNo |
+----------+--------+
| John Doe | 1001   |
| Jane Doe | 1002   |
| Jane Doe | 1003   |
| Jim Brown| 1004   |
+----------+--------+
```

SQL LEFT JOIN

The SQL LEFT JOIN is used to combine data from two or more tables, and returns only the unmatched rows from the left table (also known as the first table in the join statement). The unmatched rows from the right table (also known as the second table in the join statement) are returned as NULL values.

Here's an example of a LEFT JOIN in SQL:

Suppose we have two tables: "customers" and "orders". The "customers" table contains information about the customers, such as their names, addresses, and IDs. The "orders" table contains information about the orders placed by the customers, such as the order IDs, the order dates, and the customer IDs.

```
customers table:
+----+--------+--------+
| ID | Name   | Address |
+----+--------+--------+
|  1 | John   | USA    |
|  2 | Michael| UK     |
|  3 | Sarah  | France |
+----+--------+--------+


orders table:
+----+--------+-------+
| ID | OrderID | CusID |
+----+--------+-------+
|  1 |    101 |   1   |
|  2 |    102 |   1   |
|  3 |    103 |   2   |
+----+--------+-------+
```

We can use the following LEFT JOIN query to combine the data from both tables:

```
SELECT customers.Name, customers.Address, orders.OrderID
FROM customers
LEFT JOIN orders
ON customers.ID = orders.CusID;
```

This query will return the following result:

```
+--------+--------+--------+
| Name   | Address | OrderID |
+--------+--------+--------+
| John   | USA    |   101  |
| John   | USA    |   102  |
| Michael| UK     |   103  |
| Sarah  | France |  NULL  |
+--------+--------+--------+
```

As you can see, the query returns all the rows from the "customers" table, even if there is no matching row in the "orders" table. The "OrderID" column for Sarah is returned as NULL, because she hasn't placed any orders yet.

SQL LEFT JOIN

The SQL LEFT JOIN clause is used to combine rows from two or more tables based on the values of the left table, and the result includes unmatched rows from the left table.

Consider two tables "customers" and "orders". The "customers" table includes information about customers such as their ID, name, and address, while the "orders" table includes information about orders such as the order ID, customer ID, and order date.

Here is an example of a LEFT JOIN between the "customers" and "orders" tables:

```
SELECT customers.ID, customers.name, orders.order_date
FROM customers
LEFT JOIN orders
ON customers.ID = orders.customer_id;
```

This query will return a result set that includes all customers from the "customers" table and their corresponding order dates from the "orders" table. If a customer does not have any orders, the result will show "NULL" in the "order_date" column. The result of this query would look like this:

```
ID | name | order_date
------------------------------
1  | John | 2022-01-01
2  | Jane | 2022-02-01
3  | Jim  | NULL
```

Here's another example of a LEFT JOIN. Let's say we have two tables: "employees" and "departments". The "employees" table contains information about employees, including their employee ID, name, and department ID. The "departments" table contains information about the different departments in the company, including the department ID and department name.

```
Employees table:
+----------+-------------+-----------+
| emp_id   | emp_name    | dept_id   |
+----------+-------------+-----------+
| 1        | John Doe    | 10        |
| 2        | Jane Doe    | 20        |
| 3        | Bob Smith   | 10        |
| 4        | Sarah Lee   | 30        |
+----------+-------------+-----------+


Departments table:
+----------+---------------+
| dept_id  | dept_name     |
+----------+---------------+
| 10       | Sales         |
| 20       | Marketing     |
| 30       | Technology    |
+----------+---------------+
```

To retrieve information about all employees and their respective departments, we can use the following LEFT JOIN query:

```
SELECT employees.emp_id, employees.emp_name, departments.dept_name
FROM employees
LEFT JOIN departments ON employees.dept_id = departments.dept_id;
```

This query will return the following result:

```
+----------+------------+----------------+
| emp_id   | emp_name   | dept_name      |
+----------+------------+----------------+
| 1        | John Doe   | Sales          |
| 2        | Jane Doe   | Marketing      |
| 3        | Bob Smith  | Sales          |
| 4        | Sarah Lee  | Technology     |
+----------+------------+----------------+
```

Note that even if an employee does not have a corresponding department, the query still returns a row for that employee, with a "NULL" value in the "dept_name" column.

SQL RIGHT JOIN

The SQL RIGHT JOIN is similar to the LEFT JOIN, but it returns all the rows from the right table (table2), and the matching rows from the left table (table1). The result will include NULL values for the non-matching rows in the left table.

Here's an example of a RIGHT JOIN in SQL:

```
SELECT *
FROM table1
RIGHT JOIN table2
ON table1.column = table2.column;
```

Let's consider two tables: "employees" and "departments". The "employees" table contains information about employees and the "departments" table contains information about departments.

```
employees table:
+----+--------+-----------+
| id | name   | department_id |
+----+--------+-----------+
| 1  | John   | 1             |
| 2  | Jane   | 2             |
| 3  | Jack   | 2             |
| 4  | Jasmine| 1             |
+----+--------+-----------+

departments table:
+----+-----------+
| id | name      |
+----+-----------+
| 1  | Sales     |
| 2  | Marketing |
| 3  | IT        |
+----+-----------+
```

The following query returns all the departments and the employees that work in those departments:

```
SELECT employees.name, departments.name
FROM employees
RIGHT JOIN departments
ON employees.department_id = departments.id;
```

This query will return the following result:

```
+--------+-----------+
| name   | name      |
+--------+-----------+
| John   | Sales     |
| Jane   | Marketing |
| Jack   | Marketing |
| Jasmine| Sales     |
| NULL   | IT        |
+--------+-----------+
```

In this example, the RIGHT JOIN returns all the departments, including the department "IT" that has no employees assigned to it. The result will show "NULL" in the "name" column for the non-matching department in the employees table.

SQL FULL OUTER JOIN

SQL Full Outer Join is a type of join in which all the rows from both left and right tables are included in the result set. If there is no matching row in one of the tables, the result will show NULL values in the columns from that table. Here's an example to illustrate this:

Consider the two tables: "customers" and "orders".

The "customers" table contains the following data:

```
+----+---------+---------+
| ID | Name    | Country|
+----+---------+---------+
|  1 | John    | USA     |
|  2 | Michael | UK      |
|  3 | Sarah   | Canada  |
+----+---------+---------+
```

The "orders" table contains the following data:

```
+------+------------+----------+
| ID   | Order_Date | Customer|
+------+------------+----------+
| 100  | 2020-05-01 | 1        |
| 101  | 2020-06-01 | 2        |
| 102  | 2020-07-01 | 1        |
+------+------------+----------+
```

The following SQL query can be used to perform a full outer join:

```sql
SELECT
    customers.ID,
    customers.Name,
    customers.Country,
    orders.Order_Date
FROM
    customers
FULL OUTER JOIN
    orders
ON
    customers.ID = orders.Customer;
```

This query will return the following result:

```
+----+---------+--------+------------+
| ID | Name    | Country| Order_Date |
+----+---------+--------+------------+
|  1 | John    | USA    | 2020-05-01|
|  1 | John    | USA    | 2020-07-01|
|  2 | Michael | UK     | 2020-06-01|
|  3 | Sarah   | Canada | NULL       |
+----+---------+--------+------------+
```

In this example, all the rows from both the "customers" and "orders" tables are included in the result set. The result shows NULL values in the "Order_Date" column for the customer with ID 3, as there is no matching order for this customer in the "orders" table.

CHAPTER 4: SQL DATABASE AND TABLE

Sql Create Database

Creating a database in SQL is the first step in the process of working with SQL data. A database is a collection of related tables and other database objects, such as views, indexes, and stored procedures, that are organized and stored in a specific location. The steps to create a database in SQL vary depending on the type of database management system (DBMS) you are using, but the basic process is generally the same.

Here's a general overview of the steps to create a database in SQL:

1. Connect to the database management system: You can use a database management tool, such as the SQL Management Studio, or run SQL commands in a command prompt or terminal window.

2. Create a new database: The exact syntax to create a new database will vary depending on the database management system you are using, but generally, you will use a "CREATE DATABASE" command followed by the name of the database you want to create.

3. Specify database properties: Depending on the database management system you are using, you may be able to specify properties such as the database file location, maximum size, and storage characteristics.

4. Execute the command: Run the "CREATE DATABASE"

command to create the database. You can verify that the database has been created by checking the list of databases available in your database management system.

5. Create tables: Once the database has been created, you can start creating tables within the database. Tables are the basic structure that hold your data in a database. You can use the "CREATE TABLE" command to create a new table and specify the columns, data types, and other properties for each column.

This is just a general overview of the process to create a database in SQL.

The SQL CREATE DATABASE statement is used to create a new database in the relational database management system (RDBMS).

Here is the syntax for the CREATE DATABASE statement in SQL:

```
CREATE DATABASE database_name;
```

Where **database_name** is the name of the database you want to create.

Here is an example of how you can use the CREATE DATABASE statement:

```
CREATE DATABASE my_database;
```

This will create a new database named **my_database**.

Once the database is created, you can create tables, indexes, and other database objects within it. You can also manipulate the data stored in the database using various SQL statements such as SELECT, INSERT, UPDATE, and DELETE.

SQL CREATE TABLE

The "CREATE TABLE" statement is used to create a new table in a database. The basic syntax for creating a table is as follows:

```
CREATE TABLE table_name (
    column1 data_type(size),
    column2 data_type(size),
    column3 data_type(size),
    ....
);
```

Here, **table_name** is the name of the table you want to create. **column1**, **column2**, **column3** are the names of the columns in the table, and **data_type(size)** is the data type and size of the column.

For example, to create a "customers" table with columns for "ID", "Name", "Address", and "City", you would use the following SQL statement:

```
CREATE TABLE customers (
    ID INT NOT NULL PRIMARY KEY,
    Name VARCHAR(255),
    Address VARCHAR(255),
    City VARCHAR(255)
);
```

This creates a table named "customers" with four columns: "ID", "Name", "Address", and "City". The "ID" column is an integer data type and has the "NOT NULL" and "PRIMARY KEY" constraints, which means that it cannot contain a null value and must be unique for each row in the table. The "Name", "Address", and "City" columns are character string data types with a maximum length of 255 characters.

SQL DROP DATABASE

The SQL DROP DATABASE statement is used to delete an existing database in SQL. The syntax for the DROP DATABASE statement is as follows:

```
DROP DATABASE database_name;
```

Here, **database_name** is the name of the database you want to delete.

It is important to note that once a database is dropped, all the data and information stored in the database will be permanently lost. Hence, it is advisable to take a backup of the database before executing the DROP DATABASE statement.

For example, to delete a database named "sales_data", the following SQL statement can be used:

```
DROP DATABASE sales_data;
```

It's important to note that before you can delete a database, you need to make sure that you have privileges to do so. Additionally, you need to close any active connections to the database before you can delete it.

SQL DROP TABLE

The DROP TABLE statement is used to remove a table from a database. The basic syntax for the DROP TABLE statement is as follows:

```
DROP TABLE table_name;
```

where **table_name** is the name of the table you want to remove.

It's important to note that when you drop a table, all data stored in the table will be permanently deleted and cannot be recovered. Therefore, it's always a good practice to back up your data before dropping a table.

Here's an example of how to use the DROP TABLE statement:

```
DROP TABLE employees;
```

This statement will remove the **employees** table from the database.

The **DROP TABLE IF EXISTS** statement is used to drop a table in a database if it exists. The syntax of this statement is as follows:

```
DROP TABLE IF EXISTS table_name;
```

This statement is useful when you want to drop a table only if it exists in the database. If the table does not exist, the **DROP TABLE IF EXISTS** statement will not generate any error and the execution of the statement will simply be ignored.

For example, you can use the following SQL query to drop a table named **employees** in your database:

```
DROP TABLE IF EXISTS employees;
```

This statement will check if the table **employees** exists in the database, and if it does, it will drop the table. If the table does not exist, the execution of the statement will simply be ignored.

SQL ALTER TABLE

The SQL ALTER TABLE statement is used to add, modify or drop columns in a table, or to add and drop various constraints on an existing table. It can also be used to change the name of a table.

Here is the syntax for the ALTER TABLE statement:

```
ALTER TABLE table_name
[ ADD | DROP | MODIFY ]
{ column_name column_type [ NULL | NOT NULL ] } |
{ CONSTRAINT constraint_name [ constraint_type ] } |
RENAME TO new_table_name;
```

Let's look at an example to see how this statement can be used. Suppose we have a table named "employees" and we want to add a new column named "email" to the table:

```
ALTER TABLE employees
ADD email VARCHAR(50) NOT NULL;
```

This statement will add a new column named "email" to the "employees" table with a data type of VARCHAR(50) and the NOT NULL constraint, which means that the email column must contain a value for every row in the table.

Another example: Suppose we have a table named "employees" and we want to modify the data type of the "salary" column from

INT to FLOAT:

```
ALTER TABLE employees
MODIFY salary FLOAT;
```

This statement will change the data type of the "salary" column to FLOAT in the "employees" table.

Here's a practical example of using the SQL ALTER TABLE statement:

Suppose we have a table called "employees" with the following data:

```
id | name  | age | salary
-----------------------------------
1  | John  | 25  | 50000
2  | Sarah | 30  | 55000
3  | Mike  | 35  | 60000
```

Now, if we want to add a new column to the employees table called "department" to store the department name for each employee, we can use the following SQL query:

```
ALTER TABLE employees
ADD COLUMN department VARCHAR(20);
```

This query will add a new column named "department" with a data type of VARCHAR(20) to the employees table.

After running this query, the employees table will look like this:

```
id | name  | age | salary | department
-------------------------------------------------
1  | John  | 25  | 50000  | NULL
2  | Sarah | 30  | 55000  | NULL
3  | Mike  | 35  | 60000  | NULL
```

Note that the "department" column currently contains **NULL** values for all rows, as we haven't yet updated it with actual department names.

SQL BACKUP
DATABASE

Backing up a database is the process of creating a copy of the database and saving it to a separate location. This is done to protect the data in the event of a system failure, hardware failure, software failure, or other type of data loss. In SQL, there are various ways to backup a database, including:

1. Using SQL commands: SQL commands such as "BACKUP DATABASE" can be used to create a backup of a database. The syntax for this command is as follows:

```
BACKUP DATABASE [database_name]
TO DISK = 'path_to_backup_file'
WITH INIT;
```

2. Using third-party tools: There are various third-party tools available for backing up SQL databases. Some popular tools include SQL Server Management Studio, Redgate SQL Backup, and MySQL Workbench. These tools simplify the backup process and provide additional features such as scheduling and compression.

It is important to regularly backup your database to ensure that your data is protected in case of any issues. You should also store backups in a secure location and test them regularly to ensure that they can be restored successfully.

CHAPTER 5: SQL INSERT, UPDATE AND DELETE

SQL Insert into

The SQL INSERT INTO statement is used to insert new data into a table in a database. The basic syntax for the INSERT INTO statement is as follows:

```
INSERT INTO table_name (column1, column2, column3, ...)
VALUES (value1, value2, value3, ...);
```

Here, "table_name" is the name of the table that you want to insert data into, "column1", "column2", "column3", etc. are the names of the columns in the table, and "value1", "value2", "value3", etc. are the values you want to insert into the respective columns.

For example, suppose you have a table called "employees" with columns "id", "name", "age", and "salary". To insert a new employee record into the table, you can use the following SQL query:

```
INSERT INTO employees (id, name, age, salary)
VALUES (1, 'John Doe', 30, 50000);
```

This query will insert a new row into the "employees" table with values **1**, **'John Doe'**, **30**, and **50000** for the "id", "name", "age", and "salary" columns, respectively.

here's a practical example of the **INSERT INTO** statement in SQL:

Suppose you have a table named **employees** with the following columns:

```
id        | name          | age | salary | department
-----------------------------------------------------
INT(11) | VARCHAR(100)  | INT(11) | INT(11) | VARCHAR(100)
```

To insert a new row into the **employees** table, you can use the following SQL query:

```
INSERT INTO employees (id, name, age, salary, department)
VALUES (1, 'John Doe', 32, 50000, 'IT');
```

This query will insert a new row into the **employees** table with the values provided. After executing this query, the **employees** table would look like this:

```
id        | name          | age | salary | department
-----------------------------------------------------
1        | John Doe     | 32  | 50000  | IT
```

SQL UPDATE

The SQL UPDATE statement is used to modify existing data in a database table. It is used to change the values of one or more columns in one or more rows in a database table. The basic syntax of the SQL UPDATE statement is as follows:

```
UPDATE table_name
SET column1 = value1, column2 = value2, ...
WHERE some_column = some_value;
```

Here, **"table_name"** is the name of the table where you want to update the data, and **'column1'**, **'column2'**, ... are the names of the columns that you want to update. The **"value1"**, **'value2'**, ... are the new values that you want to assign to the columns. The **"WHERE"** clause is used to specify the conditions for updating the data. The update will only be applied to the rows in the table that meet the conditions specified in the **"WHERE"** clause.

For example, let's say you have a table named **'employees'** with the following data:

```
+----+-------+--------+
| id | name  | salary |
+----+-------+--------+
| 1  | John  | 50000  |
| 2  | Jane  | 60000  |
| 3  | Bob   | 55000  |
+----+-------+--------+
```

To increase the salary of John by 5000, you can use the following SQL query:

```
UPDATE employees
SET salary = 55000
WHERE name = 'John';
```

After running this query, the **employees** table would look like this:

```
+----+--------+--------+
| id | name   | salary |
+----+--------+--------+
| 1  | John   | 55000  |
| 2  | Jane   | 60000  |
| 3  | Bob    | 55000  |
+----+--------+--------+
```

SQL SELECT INTO

The SQL SELECT INTO statement is used to create a new table and insert data into it at the same time. The syntax for the SELECT INTO statement is as follows:

```
SELECT column1, column2, ...
INTO new_table_name
FROM source_table
WHERE condition;
```

In this syntax:

- **column1**, **column2**, ... are the names of the columns that you want to select and insert into the new table.

- **new_table_name** is the name of the new table that you want to create.

- **source_table** is the name of the table that you want to select data from.

- **condition** is an optional condition that specifies which rows from the source table should be inserted into the new table.

For example, consider the following '**employees**' table:

id	name	salary
1	John	5000

| 2 | Jane | 6000 |
| 3 | Mike | 7000 |

To create a new table named **'top_employees'** and insert all rows from the **'employees'** table where the salary is greater than 5000, you can use the following SQL statement:

```sql
SELECT *
INTO top_employees
FROM employees
WHERE salary > 5000;
```

After executing this statement, the new table **'top_employees'** will be created and it will contain the following data:

id	name	salary
2	Jane	6000
3	Mike	7000

SQL SELECT INTO INSERT

The SELECT INTO statement in SQL is used to create a new table and insert data into it from an existing table. The SELECT INTO INSERT statement combines the functionality of both the SELECT INTO statement and the INSERT INTO statement.

Here's an example:

Suppose we have a table named "customers" with the following data:

```
+----+---------+--------+
| id | name    | city   |
+----+---------+--------+
| 1  | John    | London |
| 2  | Michael | Paris  |
| 3  | Sarah   | Berlin |
+----+---------+--------+
```

We can use the following SQL statement to create a new table named "new_customers" and insert data from the "customers" table into it:

```
SELECT * INTO new_customers FROM customers;
```

After executing this statement, the "new_customers" table will contain the same data as the "customers" table:

```
+----+---------+--------+
| id | name    | city   |
+----+---------+--------+
| 1  | John    | London |
| 2  | Michael | Paris  |
| 3  | Sarah   | Berlin |
+----+---------+--------+
```

SQL DELETE AND TRUNCATE ROWS

The **DELETE** statement is used to delete rows from a table in SQL. The **TRUNCATE** statement is used to remove all rows from a table, but it is faster and more efficient than the **DELETE** statement.

Here's an example of how you might use the **DELETE** statement:

```
DELETE FROM customers
WHERE customer_id = 1001;
```

This statement would delete the row with the **customer_id** of 1001 from the **customers** table.

Here's an example of how you might use the **TRUNCATE** statement:

```
TRUNCATE TABLE customers;
```

This statement would remove all rows from the **customers** table. Note that the **TRUNCATE** statement is a data definition language (DDL) command, and as such, it is not rollback-able and you cannot use it with a transaction.

CHAPTER 6: SQL CONSTRAINTS

Sql Constraints

SQL constraints are used to enforce rules on the data in a table. They ensure the integrity of the data by restricting the type of data that can be inserted, updated, or deleted in a table. Some of the commonly used SQL constraints are:

1. NOT NULL Constraint: This constraint specifies that a column cannot contain a NULL value.

2. UNIQUE Constraint: This constraint specifies that the values in a column must be unique, meaning that no two rows in the table can have the same value in that column.

3. PRIMARY KEY Constraint: This constraint specifies a unique identifier for each row in a table. A table can have only one primary key, but it can be made up of multiple columns.

4. FOREIGN KEY Constraint: This constraint is used to establish a relationship between two tables. It specifies that the values in a column of one table must match the values in a primary key column of another table.

5. CHECK Constraint: This constraint specifies a condition that must be true for the data to be inserted or updated in a table.

6. DEFAULT Constraint: This constraint specifies a default value for a column. If a value is not provided for that column, the default value is used instead.

You can specify constraints when creating a table or modify an existing table to add constraints using the ALTER TABLE statement.

SQL NOT NULL CONSTRAINT

The "**NOT NULL**" constraint is used to enforce a column to have a value. This means that the column cannot have a "NULL" value. When a row is inserted into the table, a value must be provided for the "NOT NULL" column. If a value is not provided, the database management system (DBMS) will return an error.

Here is an example of how to create a table with a "NOT NULL" constraint:

```
CREATE TABLE customers (
    customer_id INT NOT NULL,
    first_name VARCHAR(50) NOT NULL,
    last_name VARCHAR(50) NOT NULL,
    email VARCHAR(50) NOT NULL,
    PRIMARY KEY (customer_id)
);
```

In this example, the "customer_id", "first_name", "last_name", and "email" columns all have a "NOT NULL" constraint, meaning that a value must be provided for each of these columns when a row is inserted into the table. The "PRIMARY KEY" constraint is used to enforce the "customer_id" column as a unique identifier for each customer in the table.

Here is a practical example of using the NOT NULL constraint in

SQL:

Suppose you have a table named "customers" with the following columns:

```
customer_id (primary key)
first_name
last_name
email
phone_number
address
```

Now, if you want to make sure that the "email" column is not nullable, you can use the following SQL statement:

```
ALTER TABLE customers
MODIFY email varchar(255) NOT NULL;
```

This will modify the "email" column to be not nullable. This means that whenever you insert a new row into the "customers" table, you must provide a value for the "email" column. If you try to insert a row without providing a value for the "email" column, you will receive an error message.

SQL UNIQUE CONSTRAINT

The UNIQUE constraint in SQL is used to enforce the uniqueness of values in a specific column or set of columns of a table. This means that no two rows in the table can have the same value in the specified column(s). If a user tries to insert a duplicate value in a column that has a UNIQUE constraint, the SQL engine will throw an error and the insertion will not be allowed.

Here's an example of how you can use the UNIQUE constraint in SQL:

```
CREATE TABLE customers (
    customer_id INT PRIMARY KEY,
    customer_name VARCHAR(50) NOT NULL,
    email VARCHAR(50) UNIQUE
);
```

In the above example, the "customers" table has been created with three columns - "customer_id", "customer_name", and "email". The "customer_id" column has a PRIMARY KEY constraint, which means that it must have a unique value for each row in the table. The "customer_name" column has a NOT NULL constraint, which means that it cannot have a NULL value. The "email" column has a UNIQUE constraint, which means that it cannot have duplicate values. This ensures that each customer in the table has a unique email address.

SQL PRIMARY KEY

The SQL Primary Key is a unique identifier for each record in a database table. It is used to enforce the integrity of data in the table and to ensure that every record has a unique value. The primary key is defined on one or more columns in a table, and the values in these columns must be unique and cannot be NULL.

Here's a practical example of how to create a primary key in a table:

```
CREATE TABLE employees (
    employee_id INT NOT NULL,
    first_name VARCHAR(50) NOT NULL,
    last_name VARCHAR(50) NOT NULL,
    salary DECIMAL(10,2) NOT NULL,
    PRIMARY KEY (employee_id)
);
```

In this example, the **employee_id** column is defined as the primary key. This means that every employee in the **employees** table must have a unique **employee_id** value. If you try to insert a record into the table with a duplicate **employee_id** value, you will receive an error.

SQL FOREIGN KEY

The SQL Foreign Key is a constraint used to enforce a relationship between two tables. The Foreign Key creates a link between the columns of two different tables, ensuring that the data entered into one table corresponds to a value that exists in another table.

For example, consider two tables "customers" and "orders". The "customers" table contains customer information such as name, address, and customer_id, while the "orders" table contains information about customer orders such as order_id, order_date, and customer_id.

To enforce the relationship between these two tables, a foreign key can be defined on the "customers" table as follows:

```sql
CREATE TABLE customers (
    customer_id INT PRIMARY KEY,
    customer_name VARCHAR(255),
    customer_address VARCHAR(255)
);

CREATE TABLE orders (
    order_id INT PRIMARY KEY,
    order_date DATE,
    customer_id INT,
    FOREIGN KEY (customer_id) REFERENCES customers(customer_id)
);
```

In this example, the **FOREIGN KEY** clause defines the relationship between the **customer_id** column of the **orders** table and the **customer_id** column of the **customers** table. The foreign key ensures that every **customer_id** in the **orders** table must exist in the **customer_id** column of the **customers** table, preventing orphaned records in the **orders** table.

SQL CHECK

The "CHECK" constraint in SQL is used to specify a condition that the data entered into a column must meet. If the data entered does not meet the condition specified in the constraint, the insert or update operation will fail and an error will be returned.

Here's an example of how you might use a "CHECK" constraint in SQL:

```
CREATE TABLE products (
    product_id INT NOT NULL,
    product_name VARCHAR(50) NOT NULL,
    product_price DECIMAL(10,2) NOT NULL,
    CHECK (product_price >= 0)
);
```

In this example, the "CHECK" constraint is used to ensure that the "product_price" column only accepts positive values. If a user tries to insert or update a product with a negative price, the operation will fail and an error will be returned.

Here is a practical example of using the SQL CHECK constraint in a table.

Suppose we have a "students" table that stores information

about students in a school. We want to ensure that the "age" column of the table only contains values that are between 12 and 19.

To do this, we can add a CHECK constraint to the "age" column as follows:

```sql
CREATE TABLE students (
    id INT PRIMARY KEY,
    name VARCHAR(50) NOT NULL,
    age INT CHECK (age BETWEEN 12 AND 19)
);
```

With this constraint in place, any attempt to insert or update a row with an "age" value outside of the specified range will result in an error.

For example, if we try to insert a student with an age of 11, we will receive an error message:

```sql
INSERT INTO students (id, name, age)
VALUES (1, 'John Doe', 11);
```

Output:

```
Error: CHECK constraint failed: students
```

And similarly, if we try to update the age of a student to 20, we will also receive an error message:

```sql
UPDATE students
SET age = 20
WHERE id = 1;
```

```
Error: CHECK constraint failed: students
```

SQL DEFAULT

SQL Default constraint is used to specify a default value for a column. The default value is used when a new row is inserted into the table and no value is specified for the column.

Here is an example of how you could create a table with a default constraint:

```sql
CREATE TABLE customers (
    customer_id INT PRIMARY KEY,
    customer_name VARCHAR(50) NOT NULL,
    city VARCHAR(50),
    country VARCHAR(50),
    date_of_join DATE DEFAULT '2022-01-01'
);
```

In this example, the **date_of_join** column has a default value of '2022-01-01', which means that if you insert a new row into the table without specifying a value for the **date_of_join** column, it will automatically be set to '2022-01-01'.

SQL CREATE INDEX

The SQL **CREATE INDEX** statement is used to create an index on one or more columns of a table in a database. An index is a database object that allows you to quickly locate and retrieve data from a table based on the values in one or more columns.

The basic syntax for creating an index is:

```
CREATE INDEX index_name
ON table_name (column1, column2, ...);
```

For example, consider a table named **employees** with columns **id**, **first_name**, **last_name**, and **salary**. To create an index on the **salary** column, you would use the following statement:

```
CREATE INDEX idx_employee_salary
ON employees (salary);
```

After creating the index, you can use it to improve the performance of SELECT statements that search for rows based on the values in the **salary** column. For example:

```
SELECT *
FROM employees
WHERE salary >= 50000;
```

The database management system will use the index to quickly locate and retrieve the rows with a salary of at least $50,000.

CHAPTER 7: SQL ADDITIONAL TOPICS

Sql Data Types

SQL data types define what type of data can be stored in a table column. Different database management systems have different data types, but some common data types include:

1. Numeric:
   - INT: used for integer values
   - DECIMAL: used for decimal values
   - FLOAT: used for floating point numbers
   - NUMERIC: used for precise decimal values

2. Character Strings:
   - CHAR: fixed length character string
   - VARCHAR: variable length character string
   - TEXT: used for large text data

3. Date and Time:
   - DATE: used for date values (year, month, day)
   - TIME: used for time values (hours, minutes, seconds)
   - DATETIME: used for date and time values
   - TIMESTAMP: used for storing timestamp values

4. Boolean:
   - BOOLEAN: used for true/false values

5. Binary:
   - BLOB: used for large binary data
   - BINARY: used for binary data
   - VARBINARY: used for variable length binary data

6. Other:
   - ENUM: used for enumerated values
   - SET: used for storing multiple values in a single column

It's important to choose the appropriate data type for each column in your table to ensure data integrity and efficient storage.

SQL DATE AND TIME

SQL supports several data types for representing date and time values, including:

1. DATE: used to store date values in the format of 'YYYY-MM-DD'

2. TIME: used to store time values in the format of 'HH:MM:SS'

3. DATETIME: used to store both date and time values in the format of 'YYYY-MM-DD HH:MM:SS'

4. TIMESTAMP: used to store both date and time values with a time zone in the format of 'YYYY-MM-DD HH:MM:SS'

For example, to create a table with a date column and a time column, you can use the following SQL statement:

```sql
CREATE TABLE events (
  event_id INT AUTO_INCREMENT PRIMARY KEY,
  event_date DATE,
  event_time TIME
);
```

To insert date and time values into the table, you can use the following SQL statement:

```sql
INSERT INTO events (event_date, event_time)
VALUES ('2022-06-10', '15:30:00');
```

SQL COMMENTS

SQL comments are used to add notes or explanations to the code. The comments are ignored by the database engine and are not executed. In SQL, there are two ways to add comments:

1. Single-line comments: To add a single-line comment in SQL, use two hyphens (--) before the comment text. For example:

```
-- This is a single-line comment in SQL
SELECT * FROM customers;
```

2. Multi-line comments: To add a multi-line comment in SQL, use the following syntax:

```
/* This is a multi-line
comment in SQL */
SELECT * FROM customers;
```

Note that the comment syntax may vary depending on the specific SQL dialect you are using (e.g., MySQL, Oracle, etc.).

SQL VIEWS

A view in SQL is a virtual table that is based on the result of a SELECT statement. The SELECT statement can include any combination of columns, tables, and conditions, making views a useful tool for organizing and abstracting complex data. A view does not store data, it only displays the data stored in the underlying tables.

For example, consider the following two tables:

```
CREATE TABLE employees (
    id INT PRIMARY KEY,
    name VARCHAR(100),
    department VARCHAR(100)
);

CREATE TABLE salaries (
    id INT PRIMARY KEY,
    salary INT,
    date_of_hire DATE
);
```

A view can be created that combines the data from these two tables, such as the following:

```
CREATE VIEW employee_salaries AS
  SELECT
    employees.id,
    employees.name,
    employees.department,
    salaries.salary,
    salaries.date_of_hire
  FROM
    employees
  JOIN
    salaries
  ON
    employees.id = salaries.id;
```

Now, we can run SELECT statements against the **employee_salaries** view as if it were a table:

```
SELECT *
FROM employee_salaries;
```

The result of the above SELECT statement would be a virtual table that displays all columns from both the **employees** and **salaries** tables, joined on the **id** column. Views can be used to simplify complex data structures and make it easier to run queries against that data.

SQL STORED PROCEDURES

A stored procedure is a precompiled set of SQL statements that are stored in a database and can be executed whenever required. They allow for a more efficient and organized way of performing repetitive tasks, as well as providing an increased level of security and abstraction from the underlying database.

Here is a simple example of a stored procedure in SQL:

```
CREATE PROCEDURE GetOrderTotal (@OrderID INT)
AS
BEGIN
  SELECT SUM(UnitPrice * Quantity) AS Total
  FROM OrderDetails
  WHERE OrderID = @OrderID
END
```

This stored procedure takes in an **OrderID** as a parameter and returns the total amount of an order. To call the stored procedure, you can use the following statement:

```
EXEC GetOrderTotal @OrderID = 10248
```

This will execute the stored procedure and return the total

amount for order **10248**.

SQL INJECTION

SQL injection is a security vulnerability that occurs when user-supplied input is used in an SQL statement without proper validation and escaping. This can allow an attacker to inject malicious SQL code into the statement, which can then be executed on the database. This can result in data theft, unauthorized changes to the database, or even complete compromise of the underlying system.

To prevent SQL injection, it is important to validate all user-supplied input, and to escape any special characters that might be used in an attack. This can be done using prepared statements or parameterized queries, which allow the developer to separate the SQL code from the user-supplied data. Additionally, it is important to use the least privileged account possible when connecting to the database, and to keep the database and web application software up to date with the latest security patches.

SQL injection is a type of security vulnerability that occurs when malicious code is inserted into an SQL statement, via user input. This can lead to unintended results, such as data being modified or deleted, or unauthorized access to sensitive data.

For example, consider a web application that allows users to search for products in a database by entering a keyword. The following SQL statement is used to retrieve the data:

```
SELECT * FROM products WHERE product_name LIKE '%' + user_input + '%';
```

If an attacker entered the following as the user input:

```
'; DROP TABLE products;--
```

The resulting SQL statement would be:

```
SELECT * FROM products WHERE product_name LIKE '%'; DROP TABLE products;--%';
```

This would result in the **products** table being deleted from the database.

To prevent SQL injection attacks, it's important to validate user input and escape any characters that can be used to modify the SQL statement. One common method is to use parameterized queries or prepared statements, which separate the SQL statement from the user-supplied data. This ensures that user input cannot interfere with the structure of the SQL statement, even if the data contains malicious code.

CHAPTER 8: SQL ADVANCED TOPICS

Sql Triggers

SQL Triggers are special types of stored procedures that are automatically executed or triggered when a specific event occurs in the database, such as an INSERT, UPDATE, or DELETE operation on a specified table. They are used to enforce complex business rules, maintain data integrity, or audit data changes.

Here's a simple example of a trigger:

```
CREATE TRIGGER tr_example
AFTER INSERT ON orders
FOR EACH ROW
BEGIN
  INSERT INTO order_history (order_id, order_date, product_id, quantity)
  VALUES (NEW.order_id, NEW.order_date, NEW.product_id, NEW.quantity);
END;
```

In this example, the trigger named **tr_example** will be automatically triggered after an **INSERT** operation is performed on the **orders** table. The trigger will then insert a new row into the **order_history** table with the values from the newly inserted row in the **orders** table.

SQL CURSORS

A cursor in SQL is a database object used to retrieve data from a result set one row at a time. Cursors are used to iterate through the result set of a SELECT statement and manipulate the data one row at a time.

Here's an example of how a cursor can be used to retrieve data from a table:

```sql
DECLARE @employee_id INT, @employee_name VARCHAR(50)

DECLARE employee_cursor CURSOR FOR
SELECT employee_id, employee_name
FROM employees

OPEN employee_cursor

FETCH NEXT FROM employee_cursor
INTO @employee_id, @employee_name

WHILE @@FETCH_STATUS = 0
BEGIN
    PRINT 'Employee ID: ' + CAST(@employee_id AS VARCHAR(50)) + ' Employee Name: '

    FETCH NEXT FROM employee_cursor
    INTO @employee_id, @employee_name
END

CLOSE employee_cursor

DEALLOCATE employee_cursor
```

In this example, a cursor named **employee_cursor** is declared using the **DECLARE CURSOR** statement. The **OPEN** statement is used to open the cursor, and the **FETCH NEXT** statement is used to retrieve the data one row at a time. The **WHILE** loop continues to loop until there are no more rows to retrieve. Finally, the **CLOSE** and **DEALLOCATE** statements are used to close and deallocate the cursor.

SQL TRANSACTIONS

SQL transactions are a feature in SQL that allow you to execute a series of related database operations as a single unit of work, known as a transaction. Transactions help to ensure the integrity and consistency of your data by allowing you to commit a set of operations only if they all succeed, or to roll back the entire set of operations if any one of them fails. This helps to ensure that your data remains in a consistent state, even in the event of a system failure or an error in the processing of your SQL statements.

A transaction can include one or more SQL statements, such as INSERT, UPDATE, DELETE, or SELECT statements. For example, if you want to transfer funds from one bank account to another, you might start a transaction that first updates the balance of the account from which funds are being withdrawn, then updates the balance of the account to which the funds are being transferred. If any of these statements fails, you can use the ROLLBACK statement to undo the entire transaction, ensuring that the data remains in a consistent state.

The syntax for starting a transaction in SQL depends on the specific database management system you are using, but typically you would use the BEGIN TRANSACTION or START TRANSACTION statement to start a transaction, and the COMMIT or COMMIT TRANSACTION statement to end a transaction and persist the changes to the database. The ROLLBACK or ROLLBACK TRANSACTION statement can be used to undo a transaction and revert any changes made during the transaction.

SQL transactions are a series of one or more SQL statements that are executed as a single unit of work. The purpose of transactions is to ensure data integrity and consistency by making sure that a group of related changes to the database is completed in its entirety or not at all. Transactions are an important part of database management and allow the system to ensure data consistency and reliability, even in the event of system failures or errors.

A transaction has the following properties:

- Atomicity: A transaction is an atomic unit of work, meaning that either all of the statements within the transaction are executed or none of them are.

- Consistency: A transaction must take the database from one consistent state to another. If a transaction encounters an error, it is rolled back to its starting state, so the data remains in a consistent state.

- Isolation: A transaction is isolated from other transactions and cannot be affected by concurrent transactions until it is committed.

- Durability: Once a transaction is committed, its changes are permanent and survive any subsequent system failures.

SQL provides several statements for controlling transactions, including COMMIT, ROLLBACK, and SAVEPOINT. By using these statements, you can ensure that your transactions are properly managed and executed in a way that maintains the consistency and reliability of your data.

SQL NORMALIZATION

SQL Normalization is a database design technique that helps to eliminate data redundancy and improve data integrity. The process of normalization involves dividing a database into two or more tables and defining relationships between the tables. The objective of normalization is to minimize data redundancy and improve data integrity by ensuring that data is stored in only one place and in a consistent format.

There are several normalization rules, or "Normal Forms," that a database can adhere to. The most common normal forms are First Normal Form (1NF), Second Normal Form (2NF), Third Normal Form (3NF), and so on. Each normal form has specific rules that must be followed to achieve that level of normalization.

For example, in First Normal Form (1NF), each table must have a primary key and all data values must be atomic, meaning they cannot be further divided into smaller parts. In Second Normal Form (2NF), each non-key attribute in the table must depend on the entire primary key. In Third Normal Form (3NF), all non-key attributes must depend only on the primary key, and not on any other non-key attribute in the table.

By normalizing a database, developers can ensure that data is stored in a consistent format and minimize data redundancy, making the database easier to maintain and improving the performance of database queries.

SQL normalization is a process used to organize a database into two or more tables in a way that reduces data redundancy and dependency. The main idea behind normalization is to break down complex relationships into simpler relationships. Normalization is a critical aspect of database design and helps to ensure the consistency and reliability of data stored in a database.

Normalization involves dividing a database into two or more tables and defining relationships between the tables. The relationships can be one-to-one, one-to-many, or many-to-many.

There are several normalization rules, or normal forms, that have been defined. The most commonly used normal forms are first normal form (1NF), second normal form (2NF), third normal form (3NF), and so on. Each normal form has specific requirements that must be met in order to be considered in that form.

The goal of normalization is to eliminate redundancy and inconsistencies in data, improve data integrity, and make it easier to maintain the database over time. Normalization also helps to reduce the amount of data storage required and improves the performance of database queries.

In general, normalization is a complex process that requires a good understanding of database design and the relationships between data elements. It is important to carefully consider the requirements of a database before embarking on normalization, as the process can be time-consuming and requires a great deal of attention to detail.

SQL
DENORMALIZATION

SQL Denormalization is the process of deliberately breaking normalization rules to improve database performance or to better support specific application needs. Denormalization means adding redundant data to the database so that data retrieval is faster, since it eliminates the need for multiple joins.

For example, let's say we have two tables: "customers" and "orders". In a fully normalized database, the "orders" table would contain a customer ID column to reference the customer who placed the order. If we need to display customer information along with order information in a report, we would have to join the two tables. But, if we denormalize the database by adding customer information to the "orders" table as redundant columns, we can eliminate the join and retrieve the data faster.

However, denormalization can lead to data inconsistency and higher maintenance costs, so it should only be used after careful consideration and a thorough understanding of the trade-offs involved.

Denormalization is a database design technique that is used to improve the performance of complex database queries by adding redundant data to the database tables. The goal of denormalization is to reduce the number of joins between tables and eliminate the need for complex subqueries, thus reducing the amount of time it takes to execute a query. This is achieved by copying data from one table to another, so that the data is stored in multiple places, reducing the need for the database to look up the data in multiple tables.

Denormalization is usually done in response to a specific performance issue, and the trade-off is that the additional data can make it harder to maintain the consistency and accuracy of the data. It is important to carefully weigh the trade-off between performance gains and data consistency before deciding to denormalize a database.

Denormalization is often used in data warehousing and business intelligence applications, where the focus is on querying large amounts of data rather than maintaining data integrity.

SQL Optimization Techniques

SQL optimization techniques are methods used to improve the performance and efficiency of SQL databases. These techniques help to reduce the amount of time it takes to execute a query, decrease the use of resources such as memory and disk space, and minimize data redundancy. Some common SQL optimization techniques include:

1. Indexing: Indexing is the process of adding a special data structure to a table to help retrieve data quickly. This is especially useful for large tables where searching for data can be slow.

2. Partitioning: Partitioning is the process of dividing a large table into smaller, more manageable chunks. This helps to improve performance and scalability as well as reduce the complexity of managing and maintaining large tables.

3. Query optimization: This involves analyzing and optimizing SQL statements to ensure that they run efficiently and return results quickly. This may include modifying the structure of the query, using indexing, or implementing data partitioning.

4. Materialized views: Materialized views are pre-computed data structures that can be used to quickly retrieve data from large tables. They can be used in place of a table in a SELECT statement and can significantly improve query performance.

5. Data compression: Data compression is the process of reducing the size of data stored in a database. By compressing data, databases can use less disk space, reducing I/O overhead, and improving query performance.

6. Caching: Caching is the process of storing frequently accessed data in memory so that it can be retrieved quickly. This helps to reduce the number of disk I/Os and can significantly improve query performance.

7. Denormalization: Denormalization is the process of adding redundancy to a database to reduce the number of joins required to retrieve data. This can improve query performance by reducing the number of disk I/Os, but can also increase the risk of data inconsistencies.

SQL Analytical Functions

SQL analytical functions are functions that perform aggregate operations and calculations on a set of rows in a query result, returning a single result for each group of rows. They are used to solve complex reporting problems, such as calculating running totals, moving averages, percentiles, rankings, and other complex calculations. Some common SQL analytical functions are:

1. ROW_NUMBER(): returns the number of each row in a query result, starting from 1 for the first row.

2. RANK(): returns the ranking of each row in a query result, with the same rank assigned to rows with the same values.

3. DENSE_RANK(): similar to RANK(), but with no gaps in the rankings for tied rows.

4. NTILE(): divides the result set into a specified number of groups, or "tiles", and assigns a tile number to each row.

5. SUM(): returns the sum of all values in a specified column.

6. AVG(): returns the average of all values in a specified column.

7. MIN(): returns the minimum value in a specified column.

8. MAX(): returns the maximum value in a specified column.

9. COUNT(): returns the number of rows in a specified column.

Here's an example to demonstrate the use of SQL analytical functions:

Suppose we have a table named "orders" that stores information about customer orders. We can use the ROW_NUMBER() function to generate a running total of the number of orders for each customer:

```
SELECT customer_name, order_date,
       ROW_NUMBER() OVER (ORDER BY order_date) AS order_number
FROM orders;
```

This query would return a result set that includes the customer name, order date, and a running total of the number of orders for each customer, ordered by order date. The output might look like this:

```
customer_name | order_date  | order_number
--------------+-------------+-------------
John Doe      | 2020-01-01  | 1
Jane Doe      | 2020-01-02  | 2
John Doe      | 2020-01-03  | 3
Jane Doe      | 2020-01-04  | 4
```

The **RANK()** function is a window function in SQL that returns a unique rank for each row within a result set, based on the values of one or more columns. The rank is determined by the order specified in the ORDER BY clause of the window function.

Here is an example of using the RANK() function:

```
WITH sales_data AS (
  SELECT salesperson, sales, RANK() OVER (ORDER BY sales DESC) AS sales_rank
  FROM sales
)
SELECT salesperson, sales, sales_rank
FROM sales_data
```

In this example, the RANK() function is used to determine the rank of each salesperson based on their sales. The sales data is first grouped into a common table expression (CTE) named "sales_data", and then the RANK() function is applied to each row of the sales data, based on the sales column. The result is a table with three columns: salesperson, sales, and sales_rank, where the sales_rank column represents the unique rank of each salesperson based on their sales.

DENSE_RANK() is a ranking function in SQL that returns the rank of each row within the result set, without any gaps in the ranking values. It is similar to the **RANK()** function, but unlike **RANK()**, the **DENSE_RANK()** function does not skip any ranking values even if there are tied values.

Here's an example of using the **DENSE_RANK()** function in a SQL query:

```
WITH scores AS (
    SELECT name, score, DENSE_RANK() OVER (ORDER BY score DESC) AS rank
    FROM students
)
SELECT name, score, rank
FROM scores
ORDER BY rank;
```

In this example, the **DENSE_RANK()** function is used to rank the students based on their scores in descending order. The **WITH** clause is used to define a Common Table Expression (CTE) named **scores**, which contains the **name**, **score**, and **rank** columns. The final **SELECT** statement retrieves the data from the **scores** CTE and orders the results by the **rank** column.

Ntile()

NTILE is a window function in SQL that is used to divide a result set into a specified number of groups (tiles). The NTILE function is used with the **OVER()** clause and returns an integer that represents the tile number for each row in the result set.

For example, let's say you have a table called "sales" with columns "sale_id", "sale_date", and "sale_amount". You want to divide the total sales into 4 equal groups based on sale amount. To do this, you can use the following SQL query:

```
SELECT sale_id, sale_date, sale_amount, NTILE(4) OVER (ORDER BY sale_amount) AS tile
FROM sales;
```

This query will return a result set with columns "sale_id", "sale_date", "sale_amount", and "tile", where the "tile" column represents the group number that each sale belongs to. The sales will be divided into 4 equal groups based on their sale amount. Note that the **OVER()** clause is used to specify the sorting order for the sale amount.

The **SUM function** in SQL is used to calculate the sum of values in a column. It takes a column as an argument and returns the sum of all the values in that column. The syntax of the SUM function is as follows:

```
SELECT SUM(column_name)
FROM table_name;
```

Here, **column_name** is the name of the column for which you want to calculate the sum, and **table_name** is the name of the table containing the data.

For example, consider a table named "sales" with columns "item_id", "item_name", and "price". You can use the SUM function to calculate the total sales as follows:

```
SELECT SUM(price)
FROM sales;
```

The result of this query will be the sum of all the values in the "price" column.

SQL WINDOW FUNCTIONS

SQL window functions are a group of functions that operate on a set of rows within a query's result set, and return a single value for each row based on values from other rows within the same result set.

A common use case for window functions is to calculate running totals or moving averages, although they can also be used for other purposes such as calculating percentiles or rankings.

Window functions are applied to a result set using the **OVER** clause, which defines the set of rows that the function will operate on. The following is an example of how to use the SUM window function to calculate a running total of sales:

```
SELECT date, sales, SUM(sales) OVER (ORDER BY date ROWS
BETWEEN UNBOUNDED PRECEDING AND CURRENT ROW)
as running_total

FROM sales_table

ORDER BY date;
```

In this example, the SUM window function is being applied to the **sales** column, and is ordered by the **date** column. The **ROWS BETWEEN UNBOUNDED PRECEDING AND CURRENT ROW** clause specifies that the function should operate on all rows from the start of the result set to the current row.

The result of this query would be a table that includes a running total of sales, calculated for each row in the result set based on all previous rows in the result set.

SQL COMMON TABLE EXPRESSIONS (CTES)

A Common Table Expression (CTE) is a temporary named result set in SQL that can be referred within a SELECT, INSERT, UPDATE, DELETE, or CREATE VIEW statement. CTEs are used to simplify complex and nested queries and improve readability. The result of a CTE is similar to a derived table, but unlike derived tables, CTEs can be self-referencing and can be used multiple times within the same query.

The syntax for creating a CTE is as follows:

```
WITH cte_name (column_name1, column_name2, ...) AS

(

SELECT column1, column2, ...

FROM table_name

WHERE some_condition

)
```

The CTE is defined immediately after the WITH clause, followed by the SELECT statement that returns the data for the CTE. The CTE is then referred to by its name in the main query that follows the CTE.

Here is an example that demonstrates the use of CTEs:

```
WITH customer_order_cte (customer_id, order_total) AS

(

SELECT customer_id, SUM(amount)

FROM orders

GROUP BY customer_id

)

SELECT     customers.first_name,     customers.last_name,
customer_order_cte.order_total

FROM customers

JOIN customer_order_cte

ON                    customers.customer_id                    =
customer_order_cte.customer_id;
```

In this example, the CTE named "customer_order_cte" is created to calculate the total amount spent by each customer. The CTE is then used in the main query to join the customers table with the CTE and return the first name, last name, and order total for each customer.

SQL RECURSIVE QUERIES

SQL Recursive Queries are a type of query used to work with hierarchical data. They allow you to retrieve data from a table, and then use that data to retrieve additional data from the same table, and so on. This allows you to traverse a tree-like structure and retrieve information from multiple levels of hierarchy.

A common use case for recursive queries is to retrieve data from an organization chart, where an employee can have multiple subordinates. Another use case is to retrieve data from a bill of materials, where a product can be composed of multiple components.

The basic syntax for a recursive query in SQL is as follows:

```
WITH RECURSIVE cte_name (column1, column2, ...) AS (
  SELECT column1, column2, ...
  FROM table_name
  WHERE some_condition
  UNION ALL
  SELECT column1, column2, ...
  FROM cte_name
  JOIN table_name
  ON some_condition
)
SELECT column1, column2, ...
FROM cte_name;
```

The first part of the query defines the common table expression (CTE) and uses the **WITH RECURSIVE** keyword to indicate that it is a recursive query. The CTE name is specified, along with the columns that it will return.

The first query in the **UNION ALL** statement retrieves the starting data from the table. The second query retrieves additional data from the table based on the data already retrieved by the CTE. The **JOIN** clause is used to link the data from the CTE to the table, and the **ON** clause is used to specify the join condition.

The final **SELECT** statement retrieves the data from the CTE.

It is important to note that recursive queries can quickly become complex and can be resource-intensive, so it's important to use them with caution.

SQL USER DEFINED FUNCTIONS (UDFS)

A user-defined function (UDF) is a custom function that can be created and used within the database management system to perform complex processing or computations on the data. UDFs are written in SQL or a procedural language such as PL/SQL or T-SQL and can be called just like any other built-in function.

UDFs can be used to simplify complex expressions or to encapsulate business logic that can be reused across multiple queries. For example, you might have a UDF that calculates the average of a set of values or another that determines the number of days between two dates.

To create a UDF, you define the function name, specify the input parameters and their data types, and provide the implementation code in SQL or a procedural language. Once the UDF is created, you can use it in a SELECT, INSERT, UPDATE, or DELETE statement, just like any other function.

Here is an example of how you might create a UDF in T-SQL:

```
CREATE FUNCTION udf_get_employee_name (@employee_id INT)
RETURNS VARCHAR(50)
AS
BEGIN
    DECLARE @employee_name VARCHAR(50)

    SELECT @employee_name = name
    FROM employees
    WHERE employee_id = @employee_id

    RETURN @employee_name
END
```

This UDF takes an employee ID as an input parameter and returns the name of the employee. You can then call this UDF in a SELECT statement, like this:

```
SELECT order_id, udf_get_employee_name(employee_id) AS employee_name
FROM orders
```

This query would return the order ID and the name of the employee for each order in the orders table, using the udf_get_employee_name function to look up the employee name based on the employee ID.

SQL REGULAR EXPRESSIONS

SQL Regular Expressions are patterns used to match and manipulate character sequences in SQL. They are supported by several SQL database management systems, including MySQL, Oracle, and PostgreSQL, and can be used for tasks such as validating data, searching for and replacing text, and extracting information from strings.

A regular expression is defined using special characters and symbols. For example, the pattern **\d{3}** would match three consecutive digits. In SQL, regular expressions can be used in functions such as **REGEXP_LIKE**, **REGEXP_REPLACE**, and **REGEXP_SUBSTR**.

Here is an example of how regular expressions can be used in SQL:

```
SELECT first_name, last_name
FROM employees
WHERE REGEXP_LIKE(email, '^[A-Za-z0-9._%+-]+@[A-Za-z0-9.-]+\.[A-Za-z]{2,}$');
```

In this example, the **REGEXP_LIKE** function is used to search the **email** column for emails that match the regular expression pattern. The pattern defines the format of a valid email address, including the presence of an "@" symbol and a period. The result of this query would be a list of all employees whose email addresses match the pattern.